the
cat owner's
manual

[front]

[left side]

[right side]

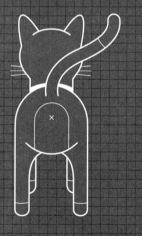

[back]

the

cat
owner's manual

OPERATING INSTRUCTIONS, TROUBLESHOOTING
TIPS, AND ADVICE ON LIFETIME MAINTENANCE

by Dr. David Brunner and Sam Stall

Illustrated by Paul Kepple and Jude Buffum

QUIRK BOOKS
PHILADELPHIA

Library of Congress Cataloging-in-Publication Number: 2004102135

ISBN: 1-931686-87-4

Printed in Singapore

Typeset in Swiss

Designed by Paul Kepple and Jude Buffum @ Headcase Design
www.headcasedesign.com

Distributed in North America by Chronicle Books
85 Second Street
San Francisco, CA 94105

10 9 8 7 6 5 4 3 2 1

Quirk Books
215 Church Street
Philadelphia, PA 19106
www.quirkbooks.com

Contents

CHAPTER 10:
ADVANCED FUNCTIONS 199

APPENDIX 211

INDEX 219

OWNER'S CERTIFICATE 223

ABOUT THE AUTHORS 224

Welcome
to Your New Cat!

[UNPACK CAREFULLY]

cat

Model: ☑ Kitten ☐ Adult
Not intended for resale

FRAGILE

THIS
END UP

Contents: One (1) *Felis catus*

ATTENTION!

Before beginning this manual, please inspect your model carefully. If any of the standard parts shown on pages 16–17 appear to be missing or inoperative, consult your cat's service provider immediately.

Whether you have just acquired a new cat or are contemplating getting one, congratulations. This product's value as a companion and source of entertainment is legendary throughout the world. Favored by everyone from ancient Egyptian pharaohs to present-day big-city apartment dwellers, the cat is one of history's most popular, most recognized brands. With proper care and maintenance, it can become a favorite with you, too.

The cat is surprisingly similar to other high-tech devices you may already own. Like personal digital assistants, it is compact and portable. Like a home security system, it is capable of functioning autonomously for extended periods without direct human intervention. But *unlike* virtually any other product on the market, it is, for the most part, self-cleaning.

While most such highly developed consumer devices come with instruction manuals, cats do not. This is a major oversight, given that their operating system is bafflingly complex, and their mechanical functions are more finely tuned than those of the most expensive automobiles. It takes expert guidance not just to understand but to properly utilize the feline's breathtakingly sophisticated software and hardware.

Hence this book. *The Cat Owner's Manual* is a comprehensive user's guide that explains how to derive maximum enjoyment from your feline. It is not necessary to read it from cover to cover. For ease of use, this book has been divided into 11 sections. If you have a question or problem, turn to any of the following chapters:

OVERVIEW OF MAKES AND MODELS (pages 23–49) offers a primer of the dozens of cat models, a quick look at important hardware and software variations, and guidance on selecting the right variety for your lifestyle.

HOME INSTALLATION (pages 51–73) explains how to safely introduce a cat into your home and to its new human and/or animal companions.

DAILY INTERACTION (pages 75–91) covers routine maintenance issues and the nuances of cat behavior, body language, and play preferences.

BASIC PROGRAMMING (pages 95–109) offers an overview of factory-installed software (instinctive behaviors) and owner-installed software add-ons (training).

FUEL REQUIREMENTS (pages 111–123) outlines your feline's nutritional requirements, including when to feed, what to feed, and how much to feed.

EXTERIOR MAINTENANCE (pages 125–142) explains how to handle body-work and detailing issues, including grooming, bathing, and nail clipping.

GROWTH AND DEVELOPMENT (pages 145–150) covers kitten growth milestones, neutering/spaying, and how to calculate your cat's physiological age.

INTERIOR MAINTENANCE (pages 153–170) explains how to monitor a cat's mechanical systems for signs of trouble and how to select an authorized service provider for technical support.

EMERGENCY MAINTENANCE (pages 173–196) lists major medical conditions that may afflict felines and outlines possible treatment alternatives.

ADVANCED FUNCTIONS (pages 199–209) surveys additional programming options for cats and offers a brief look at hardware modifications and reproduction.

The **APPENDIX** (pages 211–218) addresses frequently asked questions about common hardware and software glitches. It also includes information on additional technical support and a glossary of important terms.

When managed properly, a cat can furnish endless hours of entertainment and companionship. Remember, however, that learning to live with such a complex system requires energy, commitment, and patience. As you cope with software bugs, training setbacks, and unauthorized hair ball discharges, remember that the final result—a loving feline—will be worth the effort.

Congratulations and welcome to the world of cat ownership!

The Cat:
Diagram and Parts List

All cats have the same complement of pre-installed parts and capabilities. If yours is missing one or more of the parts or systems herein described, contact an authorized service provider immediately.

The Head

Eyes: Each model contains two. Feline irises form a distinctive vertical slit, rather than the circle common in most mammals. The visual system is protected by a "third eyelid" that deploys from the interior corner of each eye socket.

Ears: Each model contains two. A cat's outer ear can rotate 180 degrees, allowing it to scan its environment for particular sounds and pinpoint them with great precision.

Nose: The cat's sense of smell is superior to that of humans, but markedly inferior to that of dogs. A newborn kitten's nose is already so finely tuned that it can differentiate one of its mother's nipples from the others via smell.

Tongue: The hundreds of tiny barbs covering its surface are used for several tasks—including scraping meat from the bones of prey; washing and grooming the coat; drying wet fur; and acting as a temperature control system (by relieving overheating through panting and the evaporation of saliva). Cats drink by forming a depression in the front of their tongues and using it to convey liquid to their mouths.

Teeth: Felines do not chew their food; they chop it. Adult domestic cats come equipped with 30 teeth, all of which are designed for shredding meat. They use their large fangs, or "canines," to break the necks of their prey. In the case of domestic felines, these teeth are optimally spaced for dispatching mice.

Whiskers: Positioned in sets of 12 on each side of the muzzle, these thick, deeply set hairs are highly developed sensory organs. Among other things, they can gauge changes in wind direction and detect nearby movement in extreme low-light environments. They also help the cat determine if it can squeeze through a tight space (the whiskers are usually the same span as the feline's body at its widest point, unless the cat is obese or extremely pregnant). During hunting, the cat can push the whiskers forward, to provide information about the prey it is grappling with.

⚠ *CAUTION: Never cut a cat's whiskers. Doing so will prevent the cat from doing the things described above (as well as several other subroutines that are necessary for the day-to-day comfort and survival of the feline). Furthermore, the whiskers are extremely sensitive; cutting them is certain to make the cat experience pain.*

The Body

Coat: Most cat coats incorporate three hair types: a topcoat composed of "guard hairs" and an undercoat of bristly "awn hairs" and softer "down hairs." Purebred varieties may lack one or more of these. For instance, the Persian has no or very few awn hairs, and the nearly coatless Sphynx carries only a small number of down hairs.

Output Port: Products from the cat's waste discharge system are extremely rich in nitrogen—so rich that they can "burn" vegetation just as an over-application of fertilizer can.

Genitals: Females reach sexual maturity at 7 to 12 months; males at 10 to 14 months. The head of the male cat's penis is covered with spines, which stimulate ovulation in the female during intercourse.

Paws: Cats walk on the tips of their "fingers." This design feature allows them to sprint as fast as 31 mph (50 km/h). Cats can have a "dominant" forepaw, just as humans have dominant hands. About 40 percent are left-pawed, 20 percent right-pawed, and 40 percent ambidextrous.

Claws: Each paw is equipped with a set of claws optimized for climbing, fighting, and grasping prey. They can be retracted when not in use. This design option is exclusive to felines.

Tail: Used as a mood-signaling device and as a balancing aid while climbing, the tail may contain anywhere from 14 to 28 vertebrae.

Nipples: Males and females are equipped with a set of these docking ports. They are nonfunctional in males.

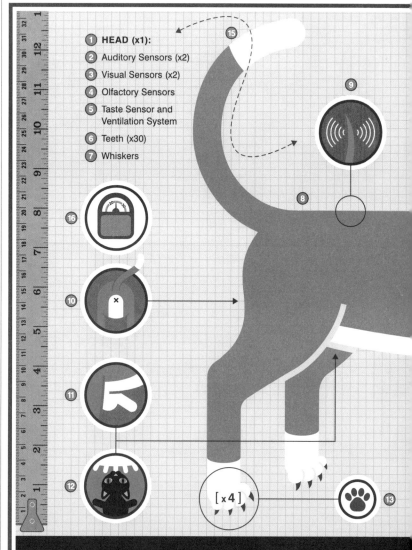

1. **HEAD (x1):**
2. Auditory Sensors (x2)
3. Visual Sensors (x2)
4. Olfactory Sensors
5. Taste Sensor and Ventilation System
6. Teeth (x30)
7. Whiskers

[x4]

STANDARD COMPONENTS LIST: Check your model carefully. If any

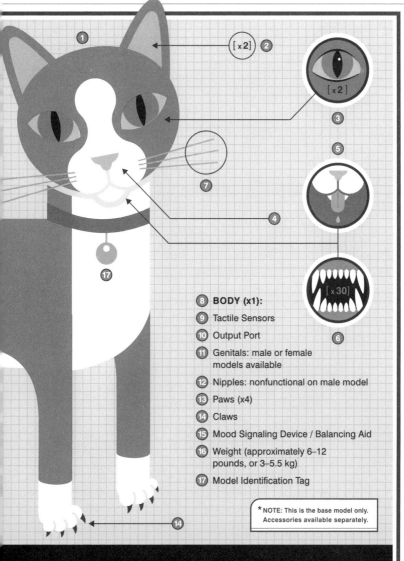

1

[x2] 2

[x2] 3

5

7

4

[x30] 6

8 BODY (x1):

9 Tactile Sensors

10 Output Port

11 Genitals: male or female models available

12 Nipples: nonfunctional on male model

13 Paws (x4)

14 Claws

15 Mood Signaling Device / Balancing Aid

16 Weight (approximately 6–12 pounds, or 3–5.5 kg)

17 Model Identification Tag

* NOTE: This is the base model only. Accessories available separately.

If the parts shown above are missing, notify your service provider immediately.

Weight: An adult domestic cat usually weighs between 6 and 12 pounds (3–5.5 kg). (See "Weighing a Cat," page 120.)

Height: Unlike domestic dogs, cats are fairly uniform in size. An average domestic cat stands about 12 inches (30 cm) tall at the shoulder.

Sensor Specifications

All cats possess a highly developed suite of environmental sensors. This allows them to perceive the world differently (often more effectively) than humans.

Visual Sensors: The cat's vision system is optimized for conditions with minimum lighting. Key hardware modifications include a reflective tissue layer at the back of each eye that increases the amount of light passing through the retinas. This causes feline eyes to "glow" at night. Cats have a wider field of vision than humans (285 degrees versus 210 degrees), but their ability to discern fine detail is only 10 percent that of ours. However, they are exceedingly good at locating, ranging, and attacking moving objects. Contrary to earlier beliefs, cats are not color-blind.

EXPERT TIP: Cats cannot see in total *darkness. In no-light conditions they are just as blind as humans.*

Olfactory Sensors: Felines carry about 19 million scent-receptive nerve endings in their noses, compared to approximately 5 million in humans. They are particularly attuned to nitrogen compounds. Since these compounds are almost always present in food that has begun to rot, the cat's ability to detect them helps it determine if a potential meal is palatable.

Auditory Sensors: Felines can pick up extremely high-frequency tones— about two octaves higher than those that humans can hear, and half an octave higher than those that dogs can hear. They can triangulate on the location of an individual sound by comparing the minute differences in its tone and arrival time at their two ears. An organ in the inner ear called the *vestibular apparatus* senses a cat's position in space and allows it to usually land on its feet when dropped.

Tactile Sensors: Each hair in a cat's coat is connected to a "mechano-receptor" nerve that sends environmental information to the brain. Although their stereotypical reputation as "loners" would seem to imply otherwise, most cats enjoy being touched. Petting can cause, among other things, a drop in the cat's heart rate and a dramatic decrease in muscle tension. Ironically, it can cause almost the same response in the human doing the petting. (See "Advantages of Cat Ownership," page 27.)

Taste Sensors: While humans possess some 9,000 taste buds, cats are equipped with less than 500. As with humans, cats respond to four broad categories of flavor: sweet, salty, sour, and bitter. Sweet makes the least impression. Because they have difficulty discerning tastes, feline culinary selections are based mostly on odors. This is why foods that smell particularly foul (to humans) can attract them so strongly.

Navigational Sensors: Many scientists assert that cats can sense the earth's gravitational field and use it to find their way, without visual cues, from one distant location to another. This feature may explain the numerous true stories of misplaced cats who travel hundreds of miles over unfamiliar territory to return to their homes.

Additional Sensors: A receptor called the Jacobson's organ, which is linked to the roof of the mouth by a duct, detects chemical sexual signals from other felines. Some cats make a lip-curling, snarl-like face in order to bring scents into contact with this sensor.

Memory Capacity

Though gauging the intelligence of a nonhuman species is difficult, scientific as well as anecdotal evidence supports the cat's standing as one of the most intelligent of domestic animals. Its situational awareness is unrivaled—as anyone who has ever watched a feline investigate every nook and cranny of an unfamiliar room already knows. Cats learn by observation; they can discover how to turn doorknobs, open cabinets, and turn lights on and off simply by imitating their owners. Kittens download a great deal of learned behavior simply by watching their mothers.

Some experts believe that cat intelligence is roughly analogous to that of a 2- to 3-year-old child. This does not mean, however, that they are easy to train. Cats, unlike dogs, are not social animals programmed with an innate desire to please their superiors. Cats are solitary hunters with only the vaguest concept of hierarchy and little desire to "please" anyone but themselves. They are capable of mastering complex behaviors, but only on their own terms. Often the only effective motivation is food and, to a lesser degree, praise.

Product Life Span

Felines are generally quite long-lived, though mileage varies depending on owner maintenance and genetic predisposition. In a handful of documented cases, cats have exceeded 30 years in age. Typically, indoor cats (Fig. A) may live 12 to 18 years, with many surviving into their 20s. Outdoor cats (Fig. B) face greater threat of accident and/or illness, and average roughly 10 years.

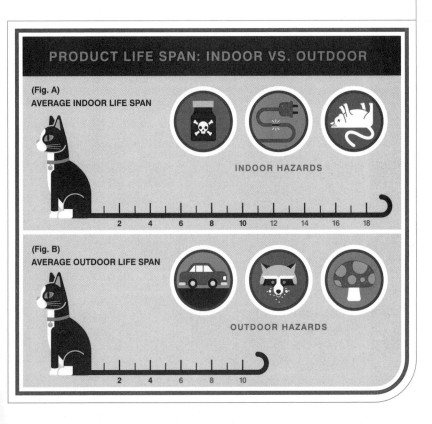

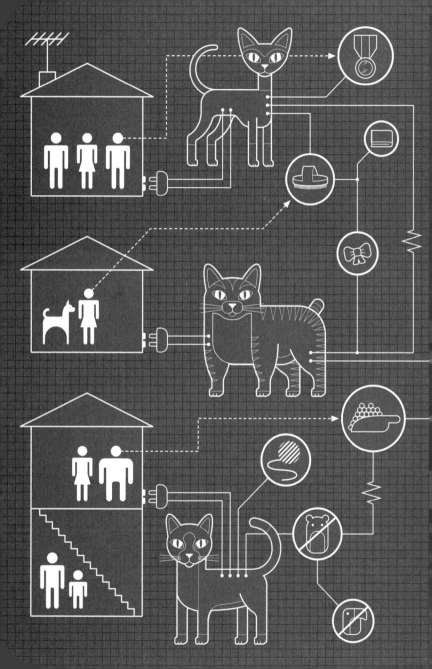

Chapter 1

Overview of Makes and Models

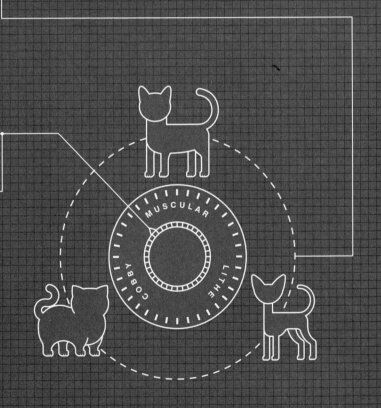

A Brief Product History

The modern domestic feline is a classic example of successful niche marketing. Descended from the African wildcat (Fig. A), it attracted human interest at roughly the same time the first agricultural communities coalesced thousands of years ago along the banks of the Nile River. The African wildcat (*Felis silvestris libyca*) hunted mice and rats, which farmers were desperate to keep out of their stored grain. The cat was encouraged to apply its "killer app" around fields and silos, and a working relationship was forged (Fig. B). Thus the feline won a place of honor in human communities throughout Africa, Europe, Asia, and, finally, across the entire planet.

Today there are some 500 million domestic cats (*Felis catus*) worldwide. Yet throughout its roughly 8,000-year association with humans, the cat's programming and design have changed little. Unlike the dog, which is descended from the wolf but in most cases no longer even remotely resembles it, the body shape and size of the typical domestic feline is quite similar to that of its wild forebears. This is because while dogs underwent intensive selective breeding to make them better guards, herders, and/or companions, cats were already optimally configured for vermin control and thus left alone.

The programming of the domestic feline (Fig. C) also remains unaltered. In fact, nearly all standard house cat behaviors are also evident in larger, less user-friendly models such as the leopard and mountain lion. The domestic feline's chief concession to the modern world is a subroutine allowing it to tolerate close association with humans. Novice owners should keep this unique origin in mind as they deal with cat behaviors that may seem, at first, unfathomable. Rest assured there is a reason for everything a cat does—even if that reason is known only to the cat.

PRODUCT HISTORY

(Fig. A)
AFRICAN WILDCAT

(Fig. B)
AGRICULTURAL ASSISTANT

(Fig. C)
DOMESTIC COMPANION

Hardware Variations

Throughout the cat's thousands of years of service, its physical template has remained largely unaltered. Only in the last hundred years has it been substantially modified by selective breeding. Today there are three body designs: muscular (Fig. A—the standard, traditional shape seen in the typical shorthaired house cat); cobby (Fig. B—stumpy legs and broad body, as in Persians); and lithe (Fig. C—extremely slim body and limbs, and a wedge-shaped head).

Felines bred to participate in cat shows often look markedly different from cats bred as domestic companions. For instance, "competition quality" Siamese have extremely angular faces and thin, lithe bodies. However, in many cases Siamese bred for home use retain their more powerful-looking "standard" body and sport a less angular face.

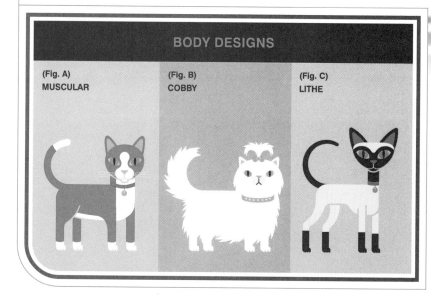

BODY DESIGNS

(Fig. A)
MUSCULAR

(Fig. B)
COBBY

(Fig. C)
LITHE

As the years go by, more and more cat varieties are becoming available, some of which depart quite radically from standard feline design parameters. Recent innovations include the Devon and Cornish Rex, which both sport wavy-haired coats; the Sphynx, which has almost no hair at all; and the Scottish Fold, with distinctly folded ears. However, the majority of the world's felines still adhere to the traditional body shape.

Advantages of Cat Ownership

Adopting a feline companion offers many advantages to human beings, both physical and psychological. A cat can provide companionship, love, and the opportunity to form an intimate bond with a member of another, distinctly different species. They offer important physiological benefits as well. Scientific studies demonstrate that physical interaction with a cat can lower one's heart rate and blood pressure. The sound of purring can also induce calming effects on the average human. A good-natured cat can help fight depression and loneliness, as well as provide endless hours of amusement. This is one of the reasons they are used extensively in nursing homes and hospitals as "therapy animals." Considering the benefits, the relatively nominal cost of maintaining a cat seems like a wise investment—provided you are committed to caring for it properly.

Top-Selling Models

Most of the world's cats are the products of random genetic combinations. These are called "mixed breeds." However, there are also dozens of selectively bred models that reliably reproduce a particular suite of aesthetic traits. Felines created in this way are called "purebreds." Roughly 40 of these are accepted as distinct varieties by the Cat Fanciers' Association (CFA), the world's largest cat registry. The following are some of the most popular, and most unique, models. If any interest you, consult a veterinarian, public library, or local breed club for more information. Always acquire a purebred from a reputable source.

Abyssinian: This model, allegedly imported from Abyssinia (now Ethiopia) to England in the nineteenth century, bears a strong resemblance to ancient Egyptian varieties pictured in hieroglyphs. *Exterior:* Extremely lean, lithe body—usually cinnamon-colored but red, blue, and fawn variations are also available. Large, expressive eyes surrounded by a ring of dark pigment. There is also a longhaired version called the Somali. *Best Features:* Extremely energetic and gregarious. Always ready to play and perform amusing antics. *Caveat: Always* ready to play and perform amusing antics—even at 2 A.M. on a workday. *Special Programming:* The "Aby" can display an almost doglike devotion to its owner. *Ideal Owner:* Anyone willing to tolerate its high jinks and provide the extra attention this cat requires.

American Shorthair: Created by a mix of selective breeding and natural selection, this model arose from the hardy farm cats who accompanied European settlers to North America. *Exterior:* Short hair in a myriad of colors and patterns, the most common being the classic silver tabby design. Strong, solidly built muscular body. *Best Features:* Sociable and easy to train. Gets along well with pets and children. Carries almost none of the genetic defects sometimes seen in purebreds. *Caveat:* Not the most affectionate of felines. *Special Programming:* Extraordinary mousers. *Ideal Owner:* Excellent for almost anyone.

Balinese: A longhaired Siamese developed from spontaneously mutated kittens in the 1950s. *Exterior:* Same color patterns as in the traditional Siamese. *Best Features:* Highly intelligent and playful. The coat is not as long as those of other longhair breeds, and it is therefore easier to maintain. *Caveat:* Makes use of the same loud, insistent yowl heard from Siamese. *Special Programming:* The personality of the Balinese is essentially the same as that of the Siamese—extremely gregarious and easily trainable. *Ideal Owner:* Anyone who doesn't mind a vocal, energetic cat.

Birman: Allegedly developed in the nineteenth century using cats imported from Burma. *Exterior:* Blue eyes, long and silky coat, white paws. *Best Features:* Fur does not mat as easily as that of other longhair models. The Birman's meow is particularly soothing and melodious. *Caveat:* It is very difficult to breed a proper Birman. Kittens are expensive and waiting lists are long. *Special Programming:* Easygoing personality; gregarious and easy to handle. *Ideal Owner:* Families with children.

Burmese: All North American and European Burmese were allegedly bred from a single specimen brought to America from Burma (where the breed is thought to be hundreds of years old) in the early twentieth century. *Exterior:* Short hair over a heavy, compact, well-muscled body. Available in sable, champagne, platinum, and blue (the European version comes in a much wider range of hues). *Best Features:* Very playful; devoted to its owner. Short coat requires minimal maintenance. *Caveat:* Loud and persistent talkers—though not as loud and persistent as the Siamese. *Special Programming:* Burmese are extremely intelligent. *Ideal Owner:* A family or individual who can provide this feline the attention it craves.

TOP-SELLING MODELS: There are many breeds to choose from. The

models shown above (and on pages 34–35) represent some of the most popular felines.

Egyptian Mau: Allegedly descended from a subspecies of the African wildcat. Its name, "mau," means "cat" in ancient Egyptian. ***Exterior:*** Spotted, leopard-like coat. Many feature a color pattern resembling a scarab (beetle) on their brows. ***Best Features:*** Highly intelligent, devoted to its family. Possesses a wild-looking, cheetahlike gait. ***Caveat:*** Good specimens are expensive and rather rare. ***Special Programming:*** Unique, perennially worried-looking facial expression. ***Ideal Owner:*** Almost anyone would find it an excellent pet.

Exotic: Developed by crossbreeding Persians with the American Shorthair, it is essentially a shorthaired Persian. ***Exterior:*** Sometimes described as "a Persian in its pajamas," this model sports a medium coat in a variety of shades. However, it retains the stocky, "cobby" body of its genetic forebear. ***Best Features:*** All the fun of a Persian, without the mess and maintenance. Also, Exotics are slightly more active. ***Caveat:*** The coat isn't maintenance free. Prone to matting, it requires a thorough combing several times a week. ***Special Programming:*** The Exotic is a bit more intelligent than the traditional Persian. Gets along well with children and/or pets. ***Ideal Owner:*** Makes an excellent pet for almost anyone.

Havana Brown: Developed in England in the 1950s, it is named after a cigar. ***Exterior:*** Short, richly brown coat (hence the name). Lithe, Siamese-like body (the Havana Brown contains extensive Siamese heritage). ***Best Features:*** Very intelligent and affectionate. ***Caveat:*** Can be loud and some-what high-strung. ***Special Programming:*** The physical characteristics of British- and American-bred "Browns" vary markedly. ***Ideal Owner:*** Anyone who wants a handsome, energetic cat.

Himalayan: A cross between a Siamese and a Persian, which resulted in a longhaired model with the distinct "point" coloring of the Siamese. ***Exterior:***

Blue eyes (on all models), stocky body, short muzzle, and long, silky hair. **Best Features:** Displays intense loyalty to owner. **Caveat:** Long coat needs regular, careful grooming. **Special Programming:** Not as intelligent as the typical Siamese, but smarter than the typical Persian. **Ideal Owner:** Perfect for almost anyone.

Maine Coon: Developed in America, it is named for its fluffy, raccoonlike tail. **Exterior:** A heavy, water-resistant coat over a muscular frame. One of the largest domestic cats, it weighs from 10 to 18 pounds (4.5–8 kg). **Best Features:** Friendly and good-natured. Energetic, but not "wired." **Caveat:** Though its coat isn't as troublesome as that of Persians, it still requires grooming several times a week. **Special Programming:** Maine coons don't meow. Instead, they emit high-pitched squeaks and trills. **Ideal Owner:** Families are perfect for this breed.

Manx: Allegedly developed from a line of tailless cats inhabiting the Isle of Man. **Exterior:** No tail. Available in a wide range of colors and patterns. The hind legs are longer than the forelegs, giving the Manx a gait similar to that of a rabbit. **Best Features:** Easygoing and affectionate. **Caveat:** Prone to genetic disorders. **Special Programming:** Above-average intelligence. **Ideal Owner:** A healthy, properly bred model makes a good pet for almost anyone.

Ocicat: A wild-looking, spotted model created by interbreeding Abyssinians, Siamese, and American Shorthairs. **Exterior:** Distinctive spotted coat with striped legs. Large, muscular body. **Best Features:** Bright and sociable. Short coat requires minimal grooming. Few genetic weaknesses. **Caveat:** Somewhat rare and expensive. **Special Programming:** Amenable to training. Will accept a leash. **Ideal Owner:** Anyone seeking an exotic-looking pet with a mellow temperament.

TOP-SELLING MODELS: There are many breeds to choose from. The

35

Manu

SPORT UTILITY FELINE

Manu

97% TAIL FREE!

★ SUPERB HANDLING
★ DUAL REAR THRUSTERS
★ MAXIMUM AGILITY

OCICAT

WILD! RARE!

The Incredible, Pettable

REX

comes with TAIL-WAGGING ACTION!

The Incredible, Pettable

REX

comes with TAIL-WAGGING ACTION!

SOLD OUT!

TYPE ☐ Cornish ☒ Devon ☐ Selkirk

TYPE ☐ Cornish ☒ Devon ☐ Selkirk

Siamese CAT

Listen TO IT YOWL

Watch IT DO TRICKS

Laugh AT ITS ANTICS

SPHYNX

CAN YOU SOLVE THIS RIDDLE?
WHAT HAS NINE LIVES BUT NO HAIR?

SPHYNX

CAN YOU SOLVE THIS RIDDLE?
WHAT HAS NINE LIVES BUT NO HAIR?

models shown above (and on pages 30–31) represent some of the most popular felines.

35

Oriental: A Siamese hybrid with its ancestor's colorful personality, but in new packaging. ***Exterior:*** Unlike the Siamese, the Oriental is not limited to a "point" color scheme. Available in shorthair and longhair versions, and in literally hundreds of colors and patterns. ***Best Features:*** Lively, gregarious companion; almost doglike in its loyalty to its owner. ***Caveat:*** As vocal as the Siamese, and just as demanding. ***Special Programming:*** Extremely intelligent. ***Ideal Owner:*** An individual. Orientals tend to devote themselves to a single person.

Persian: The most popular of all cat breeds. Allegedly descended from felines imported from Persia (Iran), its design was perfected in nineteenth-century England. ***Exterior:*** Compressed face; cobby body; and most famously, a coat of thick, glossy fur available in numerous colors and patterns. ***Best Features:*** Extremely attractive felines with sedate, laid-back personalities. ***Caveat:*** The coat requires daily grooming. Also, this model isn't famed for its intelligence. ***Special Programming:*** Persians rarely vocalize. ***Ideal Owner:*** Anyone who can keep up with this ideal lap cat's grooming demands.

Rex: Comes in three varieties: Cornish, Devon, and Selkirk. ***Exterior:*** Cornish and Devon varieties both sport a unique, curly coat—the result of separate genetic mutations in kittens. The former was found in Cornwall, the latter in Devon. A third type, the Selkirk Rex, has also been recently developed. It is available in both shorthair and longhair models. ***Best Features:*** All varieties are affectionate and fun-loving. ***Caveat:*** Prone to genetic diseases. ***Special Programming:*** When happy, the Devon Rex may wag its tail like a dog. ***Ideal Owner:*** Both families and individuals will appreciate this unique-looking feline.

Scottish Fold: All felines of this model trace their lineage to "Susie," a floppy-eared cat spotted by shepherd William Ross on a Scottish farm in 1961. **Exterior:** A genetic mutation causes the ears of Scottish Folds to fold forward and down, instead of standing erect as in all other cats. Available in longhaired and shorthaired varieties. **Best Features:** Mellow personality. **Caveat:** Poorly bred Scottish Folds can develop severe skeletal deformities. **Special Programming:** Adapts smoothly to changes in its environment. **Ideal Owner:** Someone willing to research the model carefully and acquire one from a competent breeder.

Siamese: Allegedly kept by the kings of Siam to guard the royal palace. Arguably the most recognized cat variety. **Exterior:** Distinctive blue eyes, angular features, and a unique color scheme. The body is always a light shade, while the "points" (face, paws, ears, and tail) are darker. Point colors include blue, chocolate, and lilac. **Best Features:** Extremely short coat requires minimal grooming. Highly intelligent. **Caveat:** Siamese communicate using a loud, insistent yowl. And since they are very gregarious, they use it often. Experience this for yourself before deciding to adopt one. Most Siamese also crave extensive amounts of human contact. **Special Programming:** Siamese seem particularly amenable to learning tricks and to absorbing other forms of training. **Ideal Owner:** Anyone who is willing to give this cat the attention it requires. It also helps if you can tolerate loud, repetitive noises.

Sphynx: A so-called "hairless" cat, the entire line arose from a single mutated kitten born in Canada in 1966. **Exterior:** Except for a small bit of down on the face and extremities, the Sphynx is entirely devoid of hair. Skin is smooth and warm to the touch. **Best Features:** A unique conversation starter. **Caveat:** Vulnerable to everything from cold to sunlight to allergens.

Special Programming: Quiet and friendly. Doesn't like to be held. *Ideal Owner:* An experienced cat owner who can give this rare breed the special care it requires.

Nonstandard, Off-Brand Models

The vast majority of America's 75 million cats are mixed breeds. Available primarily through such informal distribution channels as private owners and animal shelters, they usually make excellent pets. However, there are some vital points to consider before adopting. Since most cat behavior is learned, it is important to uncover as much as possible about a cat or kitten's upbringing. For instance, a kitten that was not raised around humans—or, worse, one who had a bad experience with them—will almost inevitably grow up to be a wary, distrustful cat. If such information is not readily available, the only alternative is to study the feline closely.

Except in cases of inbreeding, genetic defects are far rarer in mixed-breed felines than they are in purebreds. Be aware, however, that such defects are not very common in purebreds, either. Cats have only been genetically managed for roughly a century—and never as intensely as dogs.

Selecting an Appropriate Model

All cats are not alike. Their temperaments, physical needs, and emotional outlooks can vary widely from breed to breed, and from individual to individual. To determine which model is right for you, consider the following factors:

STANDARD VERSUS NONSTANDARD MODELS

STANDARD:

1. Available from breeders and pet stores
2. More expensive to acquire
3. Can be more expensive to maintain
4. Genetic defects are more common

NONSTANDARD:

1. Available from animal shelters and private owners
2. Less expensive to acquire
3. Poor upbringing may result in a distrustful temperament that is difficult to change
4. Background may be questionable

Coat Type: Varieties such as the Persian and Himalayan require regular, fairly intense home grooming; professional care may also be necessary. Shorthaired models are usually lower maintenance. Remember, however, that all cats (except for the mostly hairless Sphynx) shed. Be prepared for this. Even more important, make sure no one in your household is violently allergic to cat dander. (See "Feline-to-Human Disease Transmission," page 170.)

EXPERT TIP: *Ironically, longhaired cats present less complex shedding problems. While short cat hairs tend to embed in fabric and are difficult to remove, long hairs are easier to spot and pick up.*

Temperament: Common wisdom asserts that cats are aloof and distant. This could not be farther from the truth. While some feline models are not very demonstrative toward their owners (the Persian, for example), others, such as Abyssinians, can be loyal to the point of mania. If you want a purebred, take its personality (not just its appearance) into account before making a selection. As for mixed breeds, be sure to spend plenty of pre-acquisition time familiarizing yourself with the animal.

Physical Requirements: It is true that most cats require very little physical exercise to stay fit. However, active breeds need regular playtime with their owner, if only to burn off enough energy so that they sleep through the night. If you're not interested in dragging a length of string through the living room, more sedentary models such as the Persian may be a good choice.

Schedule Demands: Many believe that cats are completely independent and don't mind if their owners are absent for fairly long periods. This is sometimes the case, sometimes not. All cats need love and attention, but some need a great deal. Breeds such as the Siamese may suffer, physically as well as psychologically, if denied companionship. And no cat, even one that seems aloof, wants to spend endless days and nights alone in an empty house. It may develop emotional problems and take out its frustrations on the furnishings.

Familial Considerations: Make sure that every member of your household is committed to the decision to acquire a feline. Since a cat can live 15 to 20 years or more, owning one is a long-term commitment.

Financial Obligations: It costs an estimated $300 to maintain one feline for one year. That figure does not include emergencies or the higher upkeep of an aging cat. If this sounds too expensive, consider more affordable pets such as gerbils or goldfish.

Emotional State: Do not be "swept away" by a cute kitten and make a poorly considered, spur-of-the-moment decision that you will regret later. Instead, allow yourself plenty of time for careful deliberation. The more you think about it now, the better you will feel about it later.

⚠ *CAUTION: The decision to add a cat to one's home should never be taken lightly. Likewise, felines should under no circumstances be given to third parties as surprise gifts. Animal shelters euthanize such "surprises" by the hundreds of thousands each year.*

New Versus Used Models

One of the most important factors when considering cat acquisition is whether you want a kitten or adult model. Use the following information to help make a decision.

Kitten

Advantages: A kitten will more easily adjust to its new home and to its owners. *Disadvantages:* Kittens require a great deal of attention. They can also be highly destructive. Imagine bringing a toddler into your home—a toddler capable of vaulting onto kitchen counters and climbing drapes.

Adult Cat

Advantages: A fully grown cat's personality is already firmly established, and its destructive kittenhood is well behind it. Also, most come pre-loaded with all necessary software (for instance, they already know how to use a litter box). *Disadvantages:* The cat may carry deep-seated software glitches, such as excessive timidity. Be sure to examine the feline closely and at length before acquisition.

EXPERT TIP: *If you have decided to adopt a kitten, consider getting two. This can actually be less work for the owner, because the kittens will expend much of their youthful energy and aggression on each other. Also, the companionship will make for more well-adjusted pets.*

Selecting a Gender

Some cat aficionados assert that, in general, male cats make more laid-back, playful companions, while females tend to be more secretive and reserved. Usually, however, feline personalities are so distinctive

that sweeping, gender-based generalizations are meaningless. There are plenty of reserved male cats and plenty of playful, outgoing females—so many that your decision should be based not on alleged sex-specific characteristics but on those of the particular cat under consideration.

However, the above rules only apply to felines who have been neutered or spayed. The personalities of "intact" males and females diverge in many important, and usually unpleasant, ways. During breeding season, females often announce their fertility with loud, continuous wailing. Male cats advertise their sexuality using even more unacceptable methods. They will, if allowed, mark their territory with strong-smelling bursts of urine; roam the neighborhood in search of females; and routinely fight other outdoor males for mating rights. These behaviors can become so extreme that some intact males become impossible to keep as indoor pets.

Fortunately, neutering and spaying usually end all of these behaviors, creating a healthier, happier, more manageable pet. For this reason, it is the duty of all responsible cat owners to take this step. (See "Spaying and Neutering," page 150.)

Selecting a Vendor

Numerous individuals and agencies offer cats for sale or adoption. Often it is possible to obtain a kitten or well-trained, well-maintained adult model at minimal expense.

Animal Shelters

Advantages: These facilities are well-stocked with a wide variety of pre-owned models already configured for home use. Shelters usually screen their stock (which ranges from purebreds to mixed breeds and from kittens to adult cats) for undesirable physical and psychological traits. Fees for these animals (especially when compared to those charged by pet stores and breeders) are generally nominal. Some facilities require a waiting period, background check, and/or proof that, if necessary, you will have the animal spayed or neutered. **Disadvantages:** None. Just be sure to carefully assess the personality of a cat before adopting it. Remember that most are surrendered through no fault of their own. Their previous owner may have moved or simply grown tired of the animal.

EXPERT TIP: *Many such facilities will not give animals to people who have, for any reason, previously surrendered pets to a shelter.*

Pet Stores

Advantages: None. **Disadvantages:** Purebreds offered by pet stores are usually of questionable lineage, poorly socialized, and may be in poor health. Yet they are sold at premium prices. For this reason, cat experts advise against patronizing these establishments. At the very least, kittens or cats purchased in such places should be carefully inspected by a veterinarian for physical and mental defects.

EXPERT TIP: *Many progressive pet supply stores feature on-site adoption programs for homeless cats (and dogs) in conjunction with local animal shelters. These pets are a responsible choice for those interested in acquiring a cat. Such facilities also offer a less emotionally trying selection setting than a shelter filled with hundreds of homeless animals.*

Breeders

Advantages: A qualified breeder is an excellent source for properly raised purebred kittens. They can answer even the most detailed questions about your model's ancestry, genetic foibles, and personality. Consult a veterinarian or a local or national breed club, or attend a cat show to find one in your area. *Disadvantages:* Make sure the breeder is *qualified*. He or she should allow an inspection of the facility; supply the names of previous customers; offer detailed information about your kitten and its lineage; ensure that the kitten has received all vaccinations and medical care appropriate for its age; and include a written guarantee of its good health. If any of these items is lacking, find someone else.

Breed Rescue Groups

Advantages: These organizations "rescue" ownerless cats of specific breeds, then find them new homes. The Internet offers information on numerous such groups nationwide. *Disadvantages:* The particular cat you want may not be in your area, so adopting it might necessitate travel.

Private Individuals

Advantages: Newspapers are full of ads for mixed breed kittens offered "free to a good home" or for a nominal fee. These felines can make excellent animal companions, provided you carefully examine the kittens, their surroundings, and, if possible, their parents. (See "Kitten Pre-Acquisition Inspection Checklist," page 46–47.) *Disadvantages:* Such litters may not receive proper veterinary care or socialization. Also, such accidental breeding increases the already serious problem of pet overpopulation. If you do nothing else, encourage the owner to have the mother (and father, if possible) spayed and/or neutered.

Kitten Pre-Acquisition Inspection

When examining a kitten, ask yourself the following questions. Ideally, all of you.

○ Yes ○ No	**Inspect the kitten's mother. Is she free of major physical and/or mental shortcomings that might be passed to her offspring?**
○ Yes ○ No	**Is the kitten at least 8 weeks old? (Kittens younger than 8 weeks should not be separated from their mother and littermates.)**
○ Yes ○ No	**Does the kitten seem alert, happy, and eager to socialize with you?**
○ Yes ○ No	**Does the kitten seem gentle and amiable? (A kitten who engages in unwarranted hissing or seems overly stressed by your presence may have a significant software glitch.)**
○ Yes ○ No	**Has the kitten received all vaccinations and medical care appropriate for its age? (See "Visiting Your Service Provider," page 158.)**
○ Yes ○ No	**Is the kitten's stool firm? (A thin kitten may be malnourished or have worms.)**
○ Yes ○ No	**Are its eyes clear and free of discharge?**
○ Yes ○ No	**Are its ears and nose free of discharge?**

Checklist

answers should be "yes." Even a single "no" is cause for careful consideration.

○ Yes ○ No	Is its coat clean and shiny? Does the kitten take an interest in cleaning itself?
○ Yes ○ No	Is its breathing regular, with no coughing and/or wheezing?
○ Yes ○ No	Is its body physically sound, with no lameness or tenderness anywhere?

EXPERT TIP: *In the case of purebred kittens, it is wise to have them screened for specific genetic disorders (such as hip dysplasia, deafness, etc.) that are common to specific breeds. And no matter what sort of kitten you plan to acquire, make any sale contingent on an examination and approval by your veterinarian. Detecting a major malfunction at this early stage allows you to return the kitten before becoming emotionally attached.*

CAUTION: *Kittens are not an ideal choice for households containing either very young children (under 6 years old) or the elderly. Children can injure kittens by holding them too tightly, and a young feline can deal out severe retaliatory injuries with its teeth and claws. Rambunctious kittens can also get under the feet of seniors or puncture their thin skin with playful attacks.*

Adult Cat Pre-Acquisition Inspection

When examining an adult cat, ask yourself the following questions. Ideally, all of you

◯ Yes ◯ No	**Can you contact the cat's previous owner?**
◯ Yes ◯ No	**Is there any record of the cat's previous history and why it is being offered for sale/adoption?**
◯ Yes ◯ No	**Are you sure the cat isn't being given up because of a major personality defect, such as destructiveness? (This is not necessarily a deal breaker. In many cases, loving attention can erase bad habits.)**
◯ Yes ◯ No	**Is the cat litter-box trained?**
◯ Yes ◯ No	**Does the cat seem friendly, amiable, and interested in you?**
◯ Yes ◯ No	**If the cat will live among children, was it raised with any?**
◯ Yes ◯ No	**If the cat will live among dogs or other cats, was it raised with any?**
◯ Yes ◯ No	**Has the cat received appropriate medical care? Are there records to prove it?**
◯ Yes ◯ No	**Is the cat's stool firm?**

Checklist

nswers should be "yes." Even a single "no" should be cause for careful consideration.

○ Yes ○ No	**Are its eyes clear and free of discharge?**
○ Yes ○ No	**Are its ears and nose free of discharge?**
○ Yes ○ No	**Is its coat clean and shiny? Does the cat take an interest in cleaning itself?**
○ Yes ○ No	**Is its breathing regular, with no coughing and/or wheezing?**
○ Yes ○ No	**Is its body physically sound, with no lameness or tenderness anywhere?**

⚠ **EXPERT TIP:** *Be sure to spend a considerable amount of time with an adult cat, so that you thoroughly understand its personality. Additionally, take the cat to a veterinarian for a pre-adoption checkup.*

MODEL F-02 — *American Shorthair*

TOBY

TOBY

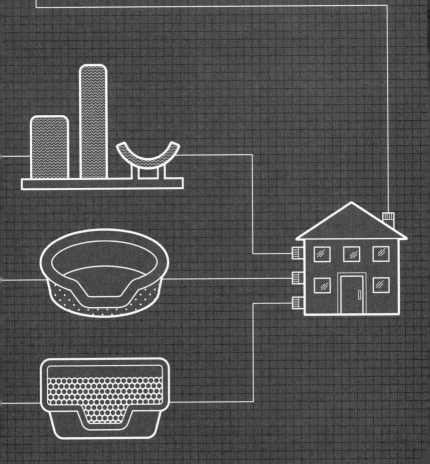

[Chapter 2]

Home Installation

Bringing a new cat into your home can be an exhilarating, albeit disruptive, experience. If your model is a kitten, you may face weeks of complex software downloads (otherwise known as "training"), plus maintenance of its complicated and ever-changing physical plant. In most cases, an adult cat will not require anything approaching this level of commitment. However, it will still need guidance as it adjusts to its new setting. For this reason it is advisable, if possible, to stay home with your new feline during its first two or three days.

Preparing the Home

Before introducing a cat into your home, it is recommended that you take the following precautions: When securing the house, put away anything that you would not leave in the presence of a 2-year-old. Remember that cats are expert jumpers and climbers and that their curiosity knows no bounds. This means that questionable objects cannot be placed "out of reach." They must be locked up.

■ Keep all medicines away from cats, especially over-the-counter painkillers. Aspirin and ibuprofen are toxic to them, as is the analgesic acetaminophen (the active ingredient in Tylenol).

■ Antifreeze is deadly to felines. Secure all antifreeze containers and clean up spills immediately.

■ Put away all cleaning products. Because cats can learn how to open cabinets, secure the products behind doors with child-safety latches.

■ Remove potentially dangerous plants, such as peonies, lilies, hyacinths, mistletoe, and evergreens.

■ Keep the toilet bowl lid down. Kittens can drown if they fall in. Adult cats can poison themselves by drinking treated water from a toilet.

■ If you display cut flowers, make sure every element of the arrangement is nontoxic to cats.

■ Secure the entrance to your fireplace and shut the flue. An inquisitive cat may track sooty paw prints all over the house. A highly inquisitive (and athletic) feline may end up on the roof.

■ Do not allow cats onto high balconies.

■ Secure all plastic bags. A cat who plays in one may suffocate.

■ Do not leave ironing boards (particularly with an iron atop) sitting out. These are inherently unstable and will topple when a cat jumps on them.

■ Fasten window screens securely.

■ Cover electrical cords in plastic or rubber runners to keep the feline from chewing them.

■ Put away small objects such as coins, nails, marbles, or anything else a cat can swallow.

■ Refrain from lighting candles and leaving them unattended. Cats are drawn to warmth and may knock them over.

■ Secure valuables that might be damaged if knocked off high shelves.

⚠ *CAUTION: Be sure to secure string, twine, ribbons, dental floss, and other such objects. A cat may ingest these involuntarily, due to the design of its tongue, which is lined with inward-pointing barbs on which string can snag and then work its way down the throat. A feline in such a situation may swallow a considerable amount of material against its will.*

Curiosity and the Cat

Felines will explore a new environment from floor to ceiling, cataloging every nook and cranny. Unfortunately, the old phrase "Curiosity killed the cat" has some validity. Cats and kittens, if left to their own devices,

will find hiding places that no owner would ever consider—hiding places that they may have trouble getting out of. For instance, cats have been known to explore the interior spaces of reclining chairs and to be injured when the recliner is returned to its upright position. Cats also enjoy sleeping in warm clothes dryers. More than a few have been killed by owners who turned the machine on without realizing their feline had crept inside. To prevent this sort of tragedy, secure such spaces when feasible and check them regularly when not.

Recommended Accessories

Commercial retailers offer thousands of peripherals designed to enhance the life cycle of standard kittens and cats. Most are not mandatory. However, the following add-ons are essential:

Litter Box: Position this in a quiet spot where the cat has ready access to it. There should be one for each cat in the household, plus an extra. Cats seem to prefer open litter boxes (which allow them to escape easily, should the situation arise), as opposed to the "hooded" variety.

Bed: Studies show that approximately 60 percent of American domestic cats sleep with their owners. If you wish your feline to sleep somewhere else, numerous purpose-made products are available. One of the most popular (at least with cats) are high-walled, cup-shaped beds with removable, washable cloth covers. These beds retain body heat and allow their occupants to curl into a tight ball.

EXPERT TIP: To cats, sleeping arrangements are a highly personal (and idiosyncratic) decision. Some felines ignore the most costly purpose-

built beds in favor of an old pillow or a spot on the couch. Once they have selected a preferred place, it is difficult to dissuade them from using it.

Scratching Post: A model covered with sisal rope is preferable to carpet-covered versions, which may lead a cat to believe that *all* carpeted and upholstered surfaces are fair game.

Toys: These need not be elaborate. Indeed, the simplest often provide the most enjoyment. (See "Games, Toys, and Amusements," page 83.)

Comb and/or Brush: Longhaired cats require a fine-tooth comb, bristle brush, wire brush, and perhaps a toothbrush (for facial grooming). Shorthaired felines need a fine-tooth comb, soft bristle brush, rubber brush, and (optional) a chamois cloth.

Collar/Tags: Put a lightweight collar on your new cat or kitten, along with a tag containing its name and (at least) your telephone number, as soon as you acquire the feline. Add tags for appropriate vaccinations as soon as your cat receives them. A "breakaway" collar, which detaches if the cat catches it on an obstruction, is a mandatory safety feature. (See "Cat Identification Methods," page 86.)

Water/Food Bowls: Each cat should have its own set. Stainless steel is an excellent choice (ceramic versions are fragile, and some felines have allergic reactions to the plastic ones). Make sure the bowl is wide enough so that the cat's whiskers do not flatten against the sides of its face (they find this unpleasant). Position the bowls in a quiet area. If you also own a dog, make sure the canine cannot access them.

FELINE ACCESSORIES (sold separately) These products can assis

Food Bowl

Water Bowl

Dry Food

Canned Food

Snacks

Leash

Breakaway Collar

Cat Litter

Citrus Cleaner

Scissors   Seam Ripper

Shampoo

Flea & Tick Bath

Currycomb

Chamois Clot

Cat Bed

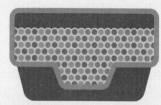

Litter Box

with the installation, handling, and maintenance of your feline.

Catnip

Jingle Balls

Bubbles

Swatting Toy

Name Tags

Teaser Wand

Laser Pointer

Furry Mice

Toothbrush

Brush

Comb

Grooming Glove

Nail Clippers

Styptic Powder

Scratching Post

Carrying Case

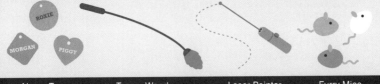

Carrying Case: Select a model with a metal grate and a high-impact plastic body. These are essential for transporting felines.

How to Hold a Cat

Most cats do not object to being lifted, provided that you make your intentions clear and handle the cat gently. Abrupt grabbing or lunging may cause the cat to flee beneath the nearest sofa.

[**1**] Support the cat's weight from underneath with one hand. Most cats will prefer to be right-side-up.

[**2**] Use the other hand to hold the cat to your chest.

[**3**] If the cat is especially large, lift it by placing one arm under its body from the back, with your hand extended through its front legs. Support its weight with your other hand. Hold the cat firmly to prevent it from freeing itself.

EXPERT TIP: If your cat bites you or deploys its claws to latch onto an extremity, do not try to pull away. This movement mimics that of struggling prey and will make the feline grip/bite harder. Instead, keep the extremity still. Without feedback, the feline's prey drive will shut down, and it will release you.

Initial Introduction

Introducing a domestic feline into your dwelling can be a fairly simple process. It can also be fraught with complications. Consider the age of your model before initiating this procedure, and then follow the steps described on pages 60–61.

HOW TO HOLD A CAT

1. Support cat's weight from underneath with one hand
2. Other hand holds cat to your chest

Kitten

Select a room in your home to serve as a "nursery." Equip it with food and water bowls, a bed, a litter box (make sure the food and litter box are well separated), toys, and a scratching post. Confine the kitten to this area until it consistently uses its litter box. Establish a regular schedule of feeding, handling, and playtimes. Children should handle the kitten during supervised play sessions.

After making sure that all potential danger areas are secured (see "Preparing the Home," page 52), allow the kitten to explore other parts of the house under your supervision. After its house-training is complete and it knows the lay of the land, the kitten can roam freely—though a heightened level of supervision is advisable during its first three months of life. Encounters with children should also be monitored.

Adult Cat

Introducing an adult cat into a new environment can be difficult for the feline, so try to make the transition as smooth as possible. If feasible, bring along some of its familiar bedding and perhaps even the litter box it is accustomed to using. Also, find out what type of cat food it eats and continue, at least for a while, to use that brand.

Upon arrival at home, give the cat a chance to drink and show it the new location of its food and water dishes and litter box (even though it will probably not use either at this time). If the cat seems particularly skittish, isolate it in one room of the house, with its food, water, and litter box, until it calms down. Then, open the door and allow it to explore the rest of the house or apartment. Do not be surprised if the cat finds a hiding place and "disappears" for a few hours, or even a day. Once it gets its bearings, it will rejoin the household.

During this initial introduction, interface with children, other pets, and strangers should be minimized. Expect some stress-triggered behavior regression, including hiding, destructiveness, and, perhaps, "missing" the litter box. In most cases these behaviors (if they manifest at all) will rapidly cease as the cat gains confidence in its new surroundings.

⚠ **EXPERT TIP:** *The holiday season is a poor time to adopt a feline. Ideally a new cat or kitten should be introduced into a calm environment and receive plenty of personal attention from its new owner. This is often impossible with decorations to put up, parties to hold, out-of-town trips to make, and guests to entertain.*

Interfacing with Babies

Introducing a newly acquired cat to an infant is, in many ways, easier than introducing one to older children. Simply hold the infant, then allow the cat (if it wishes) to approach and investigate. Then monitor the cat's behavior around the infant, and do not leave them alone together unsupervised. If the feline is already established in the household and the baby is the newcomer, the following steps will help the cat and the infant get along.

■ Before the baby's arrival, apply baby lotion and/or powder on your skin to accustom the cat to the smell. Once the nursery is set up, allow the feline to explore it. (See Fig. A on the following page.)

■ If the cat is unfamiliar with babies, invite a friend who has young ones to visit so the feline can experience them. Closely supervise all encounters.

■ Before the baby arrives, take the cat to its veterinarian. Make sure the cat is free of disease and parasites and that all vaccinations are current.

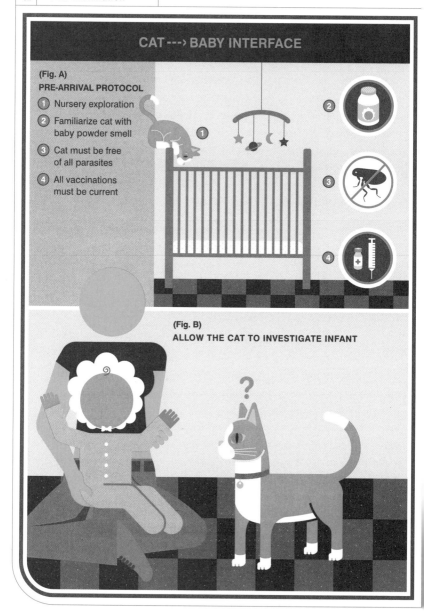

■ When the baby comes home, introduce it to the cat in the safest and most nonthreatening way possible. Hold the infant and let the feline, on its own terms, approach and investigate. Allow the cat to observe as much of the baby's everyday care as it wishes (Fig. B).

■ If possible, provide your cat with the same amount of attention (or perhaps a bit more) than it received prior to the baby's arrival.

■ Do not leave an infant and a cat alone together unsupervised.

EXPERT TIP: Contrary to the old wives' tale, cats cannot "steal the breath" of infants. However, you should not allow a feline to sleep in a baby's bassinet—as they will often attempt, given cats' preferences for soft, warm, elevated resting spots.

Interfacing with Children

Once the cat has familiarized itself with its new surroundings, it can be introduced to the younger members of the family. This protocol is different for adult cats and kittens.

Kitten

■ Before exposing children to the kitten, be sure they understand that the unit is fragile and must be handled carefully. Teach them the proper method for holding a cat (see page 58).

■ Have the child sit while you hand him or her the feline. Kittens squirm and can easily be dropped by children.

■ Responsible children can be encouraged to water and feed the kitten, to increase bonding. However, feline health and maintenance are ultimately the responsibilities of an adult.

■ Child-to-kitten contact should take place only under adult supervision.

CHILD ---> ADULT CAT INTERFACE

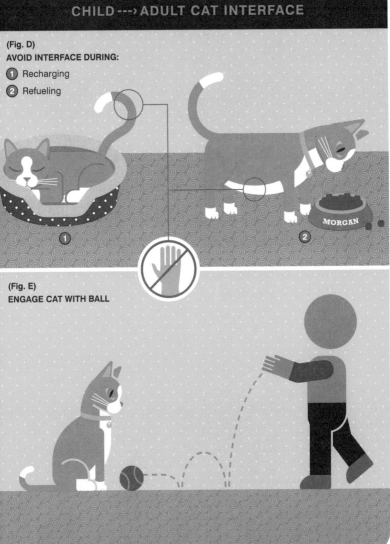

(Fig. D)
AVOID INTERFACE DURING:
1. Recharging
2. Refueling

(Fig. E)
ENGAGE CAT WITH BALL

Very young children (aged 1 to 6) should, for their own safety as well as that of the feline, have minimal contact.

EXPERT TIP: *Very young kittens aren't the best choice for households with very young children. A feline 4 months of age or older is sturdier, more agile, and better able to cope with the demands of young humans.*

Adult Cat

■ Before exposing children to the cat, be sure they understand that the unit will defend itself if it feels threatened or otherwise put-upon. Teach them the proper method for holding a cat (see page 58).

■ A "formal introduction" may not be necessary. If the children are mature and patient enough not to press the issue, the feline can meet them on its own terms, during its daily rounds.

■ If a formal introduction is required, entice the cat into playing with the children by using a ball. However, do not let the play become too frenetic.

■ Instruct the children not to allow the feline to attack their extremities, even in play.

■ Discourage children from interfacing with the cat while it eats or sleeps. The cat will not react in a dangerous way to such invasions, but it will find them unsettling.

■ Children should postpone aggressive petting, hugging, and/or holding until the cat seems comfortable with them.

■ Do not allow children to tug on the cat's tail. Also, discourage them from petting its stomach. This is a sensitive area.

■ If the cat decides to end an encounter by walking away, teach your children to accept this verdict and refrain from following the feline.

■ If possible, keep the cat's food and water bowls, litter box, and sleeping area out of the path of children.

⚠️ **EXPERT TIP:** *Teaching children how to interpret feline communication (page 76) will help them learn the cat's moods and avoid misunderstandings.*

Interfacing with Other Cats

Introducing a new cat into a home that already contains one can be difficult for the owner and for both felines. Wildcats stake out individual territories and guard them so zealously that they rarely encounter another of their kind (except during breeding season). When you bring home a new feline, you are in effect asking your current cat to share its domain. Fortunately, if handled properly, this situation can be resolved to everyone's mutual satisfaction. However, it can sometimes take weeks or even months for two felines to fully acclimate to each other.

■ Before it comes to your home, the new cat should be taken to a veterinarian for a physical examination, tests for feline leukemia and feline AIDS, and an update of all vaccinations, if necessary.

■ Confirm that your current cat is also parasite-free and fully vaccinated.

■ Upon bringing the new cat home, place it in its own private room with its food and water bowls, litter box, scratching post, and toys. Keep it there for several days, until it calms down and adjusts to you and to its new surroundings.

■ Allow the resident cat to investigate the door of the room where the new cat resides. Do not open the door.

■ After the cats become acclimated to each other, open the door slightly (secure it with a doorstop to keep it from opening too far) and allow them to meet face-to-face for brief periods.

■ Place the new cat in a pet carrier and take it to the main living area. Allow it and the original cat to interact. Feed them treats to make the encounter more pleasant. Repeat until both felines seem comfortable with each other.

OPTIMAL FELINE COMBINATIONS

(Fig. A)
TWO YOUNG, NEUTERED MALES

(Fig. B)
OLDER, NEUTERED MALE WITH KITTEN OF EITHER SEX

(Fig. C)
OLDER, SPAYED FEMALE WITH YOUNGER FEMALE

■ Allow the cats to spend time together uncrated but supervised. Begin with brief (5 to 10 minutes) encounters. Gradually increase the time they share together until separation is no longer necessary.

⚠ *CAUTION: If two cats fight, do not attempt to separate them using your hands. This is an invitation to serious injury. A loud noise may be sufficient to cause both cats to disengage. If that fails, try squirting water on them or, perhaps, tossing a pillow or article of clothing.*

Feline Bonding

Though it seems counterintuitive, keeping two cats is often easier than keeping one. Instead of hounding their owner all day or attacking the draperies and furnishings, a cat, if given a companion, will expend most of its excess energy on its associate. In order to achieve the best results, much thought should be given to the pairing. For instance, a young, energetic (neutered) male cat is best paired with another male of similar age (Fig. A). Interestingly, a placid, older (neutered) male can make a better companion for a kitten of either sex (Fig. B) than a spayed female, who will tend to be more suspicious of strangers. An older female who has lived on her own is best paired with a younger female (Fig. C).

Interfacing with Dogs

Dogs and cats are not incompatible. Often, given proper introductions, they can become good friends. However, it is important to take into account the behavioral differences of each model and how these differences can complicate such relationships. Many cats are not as outgoing as dogs and may find the attention of a gregarious, extremely large housemate to be more than they can tolerate. Likewise, dogs (many of whom are genetically predisposed to chasing small prey) may see a cat as a target. This does not necessarily mean that your dog will want to attack your cat or that your cat will want nothing to do with your dog. It merely means that their relationship—and, most importantly, their initial introductions—must be carefully managed and supervised.

EXPERT TIP: *It is helpful if the cat was socialized to dogs as a kitten, and it is* extremely *helpful if the dog was socialized to cats as a puppy.*

- If you are introducing a new dog into the home, confine it to one section of the house. Allow the cat to approach and sniff around the closed door of the room where the canine is kept (Fig. A).
- Once the dog and cat have become acclimated to the new situation, introduce them under close supervision. The dog should be leashed. Alternatively, the dog can be crated and the cat left free to investigate.
- During early encounters, offer the cat and dog extra treats. This programs both to associate their housemate with good things.
- Stroke and hold the cat in the dog's presence, and vice versa.
- Make sure the cat has a high shelf or gated room where it can retreat from the dog, if it wishes (Fig. B).
- Place the cat's litter box someplace inaccessible to the dog. Canines sometimes eat cat feces, an action that can lead to malfunction.
- Provide two sets of food bowls, water bowls, and beds in separate locations. This creates a sanctuary for each model.

EXPERT TIP: *It is not uncommon for highly territorial cats to harass puppies and/or small dogs. Often the dog can (and will) rectify the situation with a few sharp barks.*

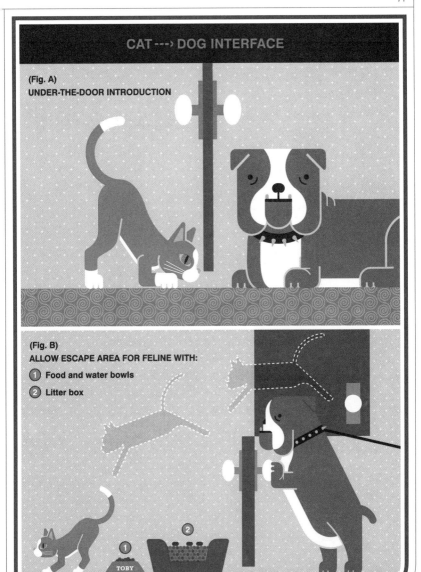

Interfacing with Other Pets

Birds: Keep smaller caged birds (Fig. A) out of reach of cats and make sure the cage is sturdy enough to withstand a determined assault. Birds can be deeply frightened by the sight of a predator staring at them; if possible, keep the cage in a location where the cat cannot see it.

Rodents: Cats are hardwired to hunt mice and rats (Fig. B), and they can never be trusted around them. Small mammalian pets must always be kept caged, preferably in a room inaccessible to felines. If this isn't possible, make sure the cage cannot be broken, or its door opened, by an inquisitive cat.

Reptiles: Larger constricting snakes (Fig. C), such as pythons, can be a danger to felines, while smaller lizards may be injured by cats. Always keep them separated.

Fish: Make sure that fishbowls are inaccessible and that aquarium tops are covered. A properly secured aquarium can actually become a source of harmless feline entertainment (Fig. D).

Selecting a Name

Given enough time, felines will learn to recognize and respond to almost any name you care to give them. However, the most effective names are short and usually end with a long "ee" sound. Good choices include Dolly, Ally, and Teddy. Try to avoid monikers that contain pronounced hissing sounds (Sissy, Sheba, etc.), and resist the urge to give complicated names, such as Alexandra.

MODEL F-03 *Maine Coon*

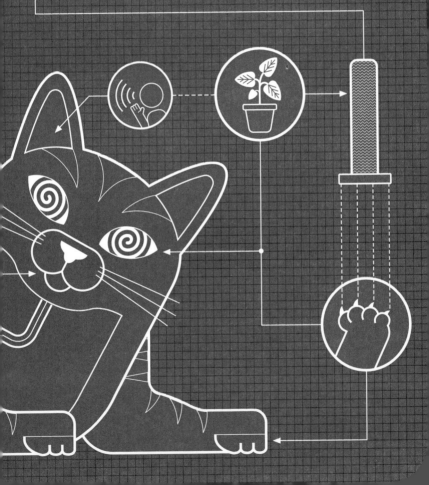

[Chapter 3]

Daily Interaction

Communication

Observing and interacting with felines can be both fascinating and frustrating. Fascinating because their actions can be endlessly entertaining, and frustrating because understanding their thoughts, moods—even litter box preferences—can occasionally become an ordeal. The following chapter will explain some of the major quirks of cat-to-human interfaces.

Audio Cues

Audible feline communication typically assumes one of the following forms:

Growl: Low-level rumbling sound designed to warn off potential aggressors.

Hiss: Another warning to potential attackers, though of a slightly more urgent nature. It can also indicate pain.

Spit: An even more emphatic warning than the hiss.

Shriek: Yet another warning to potential attackers.

Squeak: A high-pitched cry often associated with play and sometimes heard when a cat anticipates being fed.

Chatter: Not a pure sound but rather a chattering of the teeth brought on when a cat's predatory programming initiates, but cannot be implemented. For instance, a house cat may chatter as it sits at a window, looking at birds outdoors.

Meow: Standard cry of attention-seeking cats. The sound has no parallel among wild adult felines. Possibly an elaboration of the "mew" kittens utter to get their mother's attention.

Mew: A request for attention often employed by kittens. May be an immature version of "meow."

Moan: A louder, more emphatic request for attention.

Trill: An excited chirping sound that kittens and their mothers often use to greet each other. Adult domestic cats will sometimes employ this sound when greeting their owners.

Affection

Felines often use subtle techniques to display affection; these signals can be missed by an inexperienced owner. Here are the most common signs.

Blinking: Cats usually meet strangers and potential adversaries (feline, human, and otherwise) with an unblinking, unflinching stare. In the cat world, the ultimate gesture of trust and acceptance is for one model to close its eyes in the company of another. A feline that greets its owner's presence with long, unconcerned blinks or languid, half-closed eyes is signaling deep trust.

Grooming: The fact that your cat allows you to groom it signifies a deep level of trust and acceptance. In the wild, cats employ mutual grooming as a stress-relieving and relationship-building gesture. Sometimes a particularly demonstrative cat will groom its human owner.

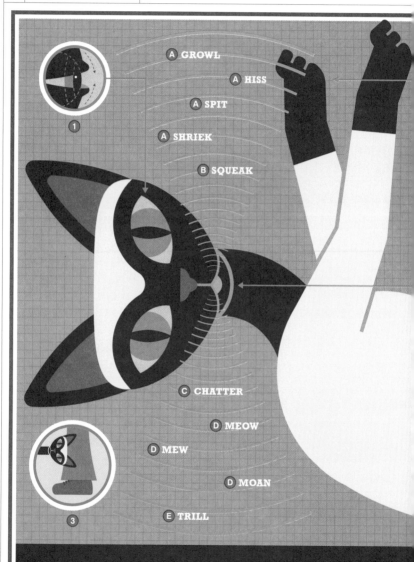

A GROWL

A HISS

A SPIT

A SHRIEK

B SQUEAK

C CHATTER

D MEOW

D MEW

D MOAN

E TRILL

AUDIO CUES AND AFFECTION: Observe your model to understand ho

AUDIO CUES:

A Warn off potential attackers

B Playful or hungry

C Predatorial noise

D Seeking attention

E Greeting

AFFECTION:

1 Blinking
Signals deep trust

2 Grooming
Relationship-building gesture

3 Head rubbing
Display of ownership

4 Kneading
Reliving childhood memories

5 Stomach display
Signals deep trust

displays trust, companionship, desire, and aggression.

Head Rubbing: Cats' faces contain scent glands that they use to mark their territory. When a cat rubs its face determinedly against its owner, it is both displaying affection and "marking" that person as its exclusive property.

Kneading: Rhythmically pressing its front paws against its owner recreates the "milk tread" kittens use during nursing to stimulate milk flow from their mother.

Stomach Display: Occasionally a feline may roll over and show its stomach to you. Revealing its soft underbelly is as profound a gesture of trust as any feline can provide. Remember, however, that this is not necessarily an invitation for you to scratch its stomach. Indeed, doing so may cause the cat to switch rapidly into defense mode.

Purring

Do not be concerned if you periodically hear a low-decibel hum emanating from your unit. This is not a malfunction, but a way for your feline to communicate everything from contentment to distress. Experts are not sure how the sound is produced. One theory suggests that the purr originates from a large vein that passes through the diaphragm. The feline may cause it to vibrate via muscle contractions, producing the distinctive sound.

Purring is most useful for mothers and newborn kittens. A mother may purr to let her initially blind and deaf offspring know where she is, and kittens purr (they begin at one week of age) to assure their mother that all is well. Cats purr while interfacing with humans to indicate their contentment or, sometimes, to ask for help. For instance, injured and/or sick cats may purr long and loudly, perhaps as a plea for assistance.

Cats and Human Speech

Though felines possess prodigious memory capacity and can store and differentiate between dozens of human words, they do not "understand" any of them. For instance, a well-trained cat does not grasp the concept that "Trudy" is its name. But it does grasp the fact that, based on previous experience, it is in its own best interest to go to its owner when it hears that particular sound. Likewise a trained cat doesn't understand that "sit" is a word, but it does understand that this audio cue calls for a specific behavior that earns a reward.

Sleep Mode

The typical feline sleeps approximately 16 hours a day, which means it spends about 60 percent of its life off-line. The cat's formerly predatory lifestyle necessitated this configuration. Their preferred prey (mice) is most active at dusk and dawn, leaving the daylight hours and most of the night as downtime to be passed in slumber. But instead of taking their rest in one stretch, felines take a number of "catnaps." Even in deepest slumber, a cat is still alert to its environment. The ears of a sleeping cat may twitch in response to sounds, and the slightest movement will instantly wake it. If the disturbance proves benign, the feline can just as instantly shut down again.

This preference for early evening and early morning activity can cause problems for owners—especially if the cat stays up half the night prowling the house or goes into a frenzy of activity at 5 A.M. The best solution is to engage the cat in strenuous play during daylight hours. The extra exertion will help it (and its owner) sleep through the night.

Proper Storage

Until recently, cats were considered an indoor/outdoor or even an exclusively outdoor system. This is no longer the case. Today, experts on feline maintenance advise keeping cats exclusively indoors. The reasons are numerous. Indoor cats are, for the most part, safe from virulent diseases; from fights with other cats; from antagonistic interfaces with dogs and wild animals; and from myriad other threatening situations. The dangers of outdoor storage are so pronounced that it degrades the performance and life expectancy of the system. While an indoor cat can be reasonably expected to live 15 years or more, an outdoor or indoor/outdoor system will be lucky to last 10 years. The disparity has not gone unnoticed by animal shelters, an increasing number of which will not release felines to applicants unless they sign a written agreement to keep the cats exclusively indoors.

Ideally, a newly acquired kitten should be raised as an indoor-only cat. This is, in most cases, the simplest way to program a feline for this lifestyle. However, if you acquire an adult cat, there are many techniques by which it can be habituated to life inside. The key is to make sure your feline can find as much stimulation, pleasure, and comfort indoors as it would outdoors.

EXPERT TIP: *If your cat makes a habit of trying to bolt out open doors, the first step is to make sure the feline never succeeds. If it does, the temptation to repeat the behavior will be strongly reinforced. Coach children to be mindful of the cat, and never access an exterior door while your arms are laden with packages. You will be unable to foil an escape attempt.*

Exercise and Play

Though the cat's lifestyle seems quite sedentary, many models remain lithe and trim their entire lives. Some experts theorize that felines may get all the exercise they need from their post-nap stretching rituals. However, a wise owner still sets aside playtime with his or her feline. These sessions both increase bonding and exhaust excess feline energy that might otherwise be used to harass the family dog or to climb the curtains. Keep play sessions brief (10 to 15 minutes). Cats are designed for short bursts of intense activity, not marathons. Often, a cat will signal its fatigue by losing interest and departing the play area. When the session ends, lock most of the toys away. This will prevent the cat from losing them under the furniture or tearing them apart.

Games, Toys, and Amusements

Because of their innate curiosity, cats can turn virtually any household item into a game, toy, or amusement. Sometimes, such play can lead to the destruction of valuable personal property. To prevent this, try any of the following activities.

■ One of the best cat toys is a piece of string tied securely to a stick (see Fig. A, next page). Users can amuse the cat while remaining seated in a chair.

■ Place Ping-Pong balls in an empty bathtub and let your cat bat them around (see Fig. B, next page). This game is particularly exciting for kittens and younger cats.

■ Some felines enjoy exploring paper bags and boxes. Avoid bags with handles (cats can catch their necks in the loops) and never risk suffocation with plastic bags.

GAMES AND AMUSEMENTS

(Fig. A)
STRING ON A STICK

(Fig. B)
PING-PONG BALLS

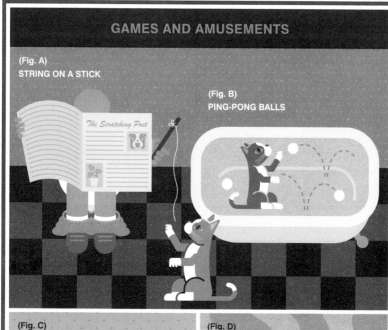

(Fig. C)
WINDOW PERCH

(Fig. D)
CATNIP

■ Cats will stalk and pursue a point of light played along the walls and floor of a darkened room. Try laser pointers and/or flashlights.

■ A window perch positioned within sight of an outdoor bird feeder provides endless passive entertainment (Fig. C).

⚠ **CAUTION:** *Avoid play objects that are small enough to be swallowed, and don't allow unsupervised play with anything incorporating string, ribbon, twine, etc. Check store-purchased toys for pieces that might detach and be ingested. It is also wise to watch a cat as it plays with a new toy, to see if any unexpected problems arise.*

⚠ **EXPERT TIP:** *When playing with a kitten or cat, always direct its playful aggression toward toys. Never allow them to pounce or smack at your hands or other extremities. They may get the message that launching attacks on unsuspecting humans is acceptable behavior.*

Catnip

Many cats enjoy interacting with catnip-stuffed toys. Catnip (*Nepeta cataria*) is a member of the mint family. This common herb, also called "catmint," affects felines in much the same way that marijuana does humans. An exposed cat will spend about 10 minutes rubbing against the source of the catnip, obviously in great pleasure (Fig. D). Then the interlude ends with the cat (according to the latest scientific studies) suffering no short-term or long-term ill effects. All feline models, including lions, are susceptible to catnip (the herbs valerian and Canadian honeysuckle produce a similar reaction). However, not all individuals are affected. Only 50 percent to 60 percent of adult cats react to catnip, and kittens younger than 2 months are indifferent to it.

Cat Identification Methods

Ideally, even indoor cats should wear a collar, with identification tags attached, at all times. This is because unforeseen circumstances could land even the most homebound feline out on the street. To assure that it makes its way home safely, its tag should include your name, address, and home and work telephone numbers. The cat's rabies vaccination and license tags (stamped with your veterinarian's name and telephone number) should also be included. In many areas this is mandatory. However, given cats' talents for slipping out of collars (and the practice of fitting them with breakaway models, which won't choke them if caught on something), tags are not the only (or even best) ID method. Cats can also be tattooed or have a microchip installed. The microchip, about the size of a grain of rice, is injected just under the skin between the shoulder blades. When scanned, it yields information that assists the cat's finder in locating its owner. Chip scanners are used at most lost-cat intake centers, including humane societies, city pounds, and veterinary hospitals. However, a "chipped" cat should still wear a collar for identification.

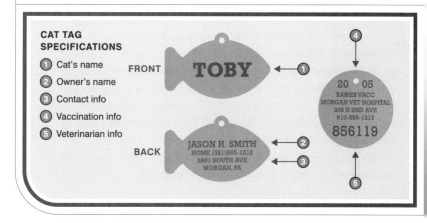

CAT TAG
SPECIFICATIONS
1 Cat's name
2 Owner's name
3 Contact info
4 Vaccination info
5 Veterinarian info

FRONT **TOBY** ← 1

20 05
RABIES VACC
MORGAN VET HOSPITAL
306 N 2ND AVE
910-555-1313
856119

BACK JASON H. SMITH ← 2
HOME (321)555-1212
2801 SOUTH AVE
MORGAN, PA ← 3

Waste Disposal Protocols

One of the cat's strongest selling points is the fact that it is largely a self-cleaning unit. The feline washes and combs its own fur and is also hardwired not only to eliminate bodily wastes in one convenient location, but to also conceal the material. In most cases adult cats come preprogrammed for litter box use. House-training is simply a matter of showing them where the box is located, then making sure they use it. Kittens have an inborn propensity for burying their waste—a propensity that is reinforced and refined when the kitten observes its mother. Given these facts, "teaching" this technique to a newly adopted kitten may be unnecessary. Simply place a litter box in the room that serves as its initial home and observe. If it doesn't use the unit on its own, then make a point of placing it in the container whenever it seems about to download (the kitten will squat and raise its tail). Carefully clean "accident" areas, because cats reuse spots they have previously visited.

EXPERT TIP: *Ideally there should be one litter box on every level of your home, or one more than the total number of cats you possess.*

Dealing with Unauthorized Downloads

Well-trained felines have few, if any, accidents, but the ones they *do* have can be extremely distasteful. Cat urine contains high concentrations of ammonia, which makes its smell particularly annoying to humans—and particularly difficult to expunge from furnishings. Yet the odor must be removed, or the cat will be strongly tempted to use the spot again. First, wash the area with carbonated water or soapy water, and then rinse. Further usage may be deterred by applying a misting of vinegar

POSSIBLE CAUSES:

1. Litter brand change
2. Poorly designed litter box
3. Poorly maintained litter box
4. Medical conditions
5. Territorial marking
6. Poorly positioned litter box
7. Psychological disorder

CLEANUP:

8. Citrus-based cleaner
9. UV light locates spots
10. Food bowl may prevent future visits

NEW FRESH SCOOP

UNAUTHORIZED DOWNLOADS: Failure of the feline to utilize the litter bo

or waste disposal may be caused by any number of problems.

or mouthwash to the spot, both of which cats find distasteful. A citrus-based cleaning product is also helpful, because cats hate citrus smells. Also, placing the cat's food dish on the spot will prevent further visits. Another alternative is to use a commercially prepared pet-odor-removing product, or a pheromone spray that dissuades a cat from repeatedly marking the same location.

⚠ *CAUTION: Never use an ammonia-based cleaning product. The scent is similar to cat urine and will only exacerbate the problem.*

💡 *EXPERT TIP: During cleanup, shine an ultraviolet (black) light on the spot in question. Deposits of cat urine will fluoresce, making them easier to detect.*

Reasons for Litter Box Mishaps

Feline house-training glitches can occur for any number of reasons, including physical illness. If the problem has no obvious cause and continues for more than a few days, consult your veterinarian. Common causes of litter "accidents" include:

Territorial Marking: Non-neutered males will often mark their territories with sprays of urine, usually deposited on vertical surfaces. In some cases this behavior may be adopted by neutered males and occasionally females. Spraying behaviors can often be initiated when a cat is made to feel insecure—for instance, by the arrival of a new cat or some other addition to the household.

Litter Brand Change: Felines can become extremely upset if their familiar brand of litter is changed to one with an unfamiliar consistency or—far worse—scent. Cats are actually repelled by the scent of strongly perfumed varieties, and they may refuse to use them.

Poorly Positioned Litter Box: A cat may reject a litter box that is in a noisy, high-traffic area offering little privacy. Relocating the box may remedy the problem.

Poorly Designed Litter Box: Some cats refuse to use hooded litter boxes, perhaps because they feel trapped while inside. Kittens may have trouble climbing into high-sided models.

Poorly Maintained Litter Box: Litter should be cleaned or scooped daily. A feline may reject an odorous or overused box.

Medical Conditions: A range of malfunctions, including diabetes or kidney and bladder conditions, can cause urine regulation issues. Intestinal parasites can trigger unauthorized feces downloads.

Psychological Disorder: A bored, depressed, lonely, or spiteful cat may sometimes "miss" its litter box.

Scratching

All cat owners must contend with the fact that cats regularly exercise their claws—ideally on their scratching post, but sometimes on such inappropriate targets as chairs, curtains, and door frames. This is not a sharpening ritual. Feline claws retract when not in use, and thus do not grow dull from contact with the ground. Cats scratch to shed worn bits of nail (which can be found in abundance at favorite scratching spots) and to mark their territory. Leaving visible scratches serves as a visual reminder of another cat's presence. Glands in the paws also leave behind a scent signature.

If your cat scratches an inappropriate object, the following steps may end the problem:

[1] Purchase or make a scratching post. Make sure it is covered with sisal or some other material that doesn't resemble carpet or upholstery.

[2] Rub the post with catnip (this will not work on very young kittens, who have no interest in this herb).

[3] Introduce the cat to the post. Scratch your own fingers across its surface until the cat gets the idea.

[4] If the cat is attacking a particular piece of furniture, position the post in front of that object. Then, secure the afflicted spot from further attack by covering it with double-sided tape (felines are repelled by the sticky texture).

[5] If you see the cat attacking unauthorized surfaces, guide it to the scratching post.

EXPERT TIP: *Shouting at a feline or using corporal punishment has no effect—or, at least, not the desired effect. Only positive reinforcement and behavior modification will sway a cat.*

SCRATCHING POST INSTALLATION

1. Choose sisal material, not carpet
2. Rub post with catnip
3. Demonstrate use to cat

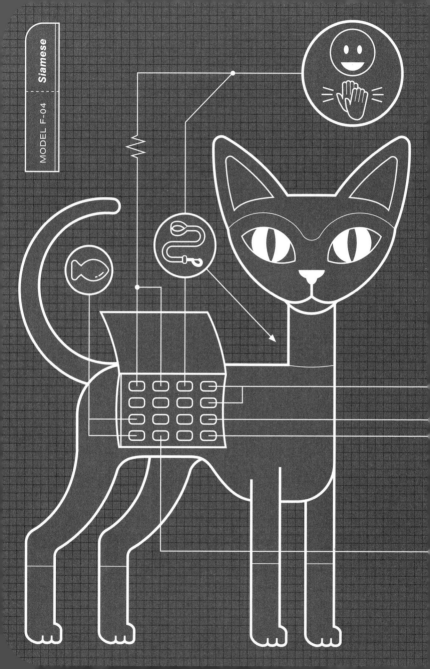

MODEL F-04 · *Siamese*

Chapter 4

Basic
Programming

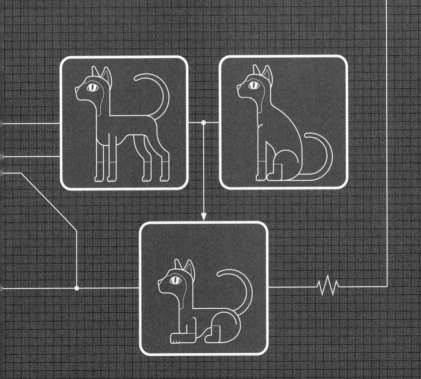

Overview of Factory-Installed Software

Each cat comes with a great deal of pre-installed programming, most of which is very similar (if not identical) to the routines and subroutines used by such completely autonomous feline systems as the leopard, tiger, and cougar. Ironically, many of these functions, which were originally designed to help the cat survive as a solitary hunter, have also eased its passage into domesticity. Here are some of the key points.

Socialization: Most cat models rarely mingle in the wild, except for procreation or combat. This rejection of group living has many repercussions in a domestic setting. On the one hand, cats can make do with much less personal attention than, say, a canine. On the other, they have little interest in ingratiating themselves to their human masters. A cat's loyalty has to be won, and sometimes it does not come easily.

Communication: Because they lead solitary lives, the means of expression at a feline's disposal are not as versatile or extensive as those available to canines, whose survival depends on communicating in a group setting. For instance, while a dog can employ a nearly endless array of facial expressions, rigid feline faces are more restricted in their ability to transmit data. Body postures and audio cues may be called upon to reinforce important messages.

Hunting: When it comes to hunting small game, the cat is without peer in the animal world. Indeed, this important function has shaped almost every aspect of its programming. The feline is attracted to a piece of twitching string because its vision is optimized for spotting small moving targets; it sleeps most of the day because its predatory skills make lengthy, strenuous exertion unnecessary; and it prowls at night and in the early morning because that is its traditional stalking time.

Territoriality: Each cat has its own territory. It is the need to patrol and defend this expanse of ground that gives them their extraordinary situational awareness—their famous "curiosity." No detail of their turf, whether it be a stretch of African savanna or a two-bedroom bungalow, escapes notice and investigation. This is one of the reasons why cats can be traumatized by a move to a new home, the addition of a new person to the household, or even rearrangement of the furniture in the living room.

Dominance: Though cats are primarily solitary animals, issues of social hierarchy come into play during mating (where the strongest male usually wins) and territorial struggles (in which the most able feline appropriates the choicest domain). Glimmers of this can be seen in many odd aspects of cat behavior—for instance, burying feces to keep them from attracting predators, but also as a sign of subordination to other cats. When cats live together, it is not unusual for the dominant feline to leave its feces uncovered as a symbol of its status.

Self-Grooming Protocols

One of the most useful bits of built-in feline programming (next to the predisposition for litter box use) is the propensity for grooming. Recent studies indicate that the typical cat spends at least 15 percent of its time in this pursuit. The procedure is identical from one cat to the next and begins with licking the front paws until wet, then raking them over the head. The feline then progresses down its body, ending with

A:/SOCIALIZATION

B:/COMMUNICATION

[FRIGHTENED]

[ANNOYED]

[RELAXED]

FACTORY-INSTALLED SOFTWARE: Most cats include numerou

C:/HUNTING

D:/TERRITORIALITY

E:/DOMINANCE

re-installed software applications.

a thorough licking of the tail. It is important to remember, however, that this is not a *fully* autonomous function. Longhaired felines require human intervention to adequately maintain their coats, and short-haired cats may develop fur balls from ingesting too much hair during this process. (See "Hair Balls," page 142.)

⚠️ *CAUTION: If your cat stops grooming itself, consult a veterinarian. This may indicate a major malfunction. Likewise, a feline who grooms itself excessively may be manifesting a psychological disorder.*

Training Options (Software Add-Ons)

Contrary to popular belief, it is entirely possible to train most cats. Though some breeds, such as Persians, are generally not amenable to this, the typical feline can be coaxed into mastering new behaviors. But given the cat's unique programming, only one approach will work— positive reinforcement. While a cat will not learn a trick out of fear or just to "please" you, it is capable of downloading complex behaviors if you make it worth its while. For instance, most felines quickly train themselves to "come" when they hear an electric can opener. This sort of conditioning can be applied to myriad other tasks.

Socialization

While many owners are perfectly satisfied with the baseline feline programming package and opt out of software add-ons, one particular bit of code is vital to the cat's happiness and yours. It is absolutely essential that kittens (starting as early as 2 weeks of age) meet and grow accustomed to humans. If they don't, the results can be disastrous. Appreciating (or at least tolerating) the company of people is an entirely learned behavior. Kittens who are raised without such contact will grow into unmanageable adults who are either utterly indifferent to or actively fearful of humanity. To build an appropriate bond, kittens should receive regular, brief, positive human contact—one or two 15-minute holding, stroking, and/or play sessions daily. It is also advisable to introduce the kitten to dogs (page 69) and children (page 63)—though again in nonthreatening ways. *If you adopt a kitten, make sure it has been properly socialized.*

Training Tips

These techniques will make even the most complex and demanding downloads easier to execute.

■ Use food treats to encourage your cat to perform. Praise, especially at the beginning of a difficult download, will usually not be enough to initiate the desired behavior. Later, after the behavior has been mastered, the feline can often be weaned away from its treat reward.

■ To encourage compliance, schedule training sessions just before mealtimes. Food rewards will seem even more enticing.

■ Conduct training in a quiet area free of distractions.

■ Keep training sessions short—10 to 15 minutes.

■ Use the same command word, such as "sit," every time a particular behavior is exhibited. Varying the command word will cause confusion.

■ If the cat becomes uncooperative, stop the session and try the next day.

■ Teach only one behavior at a time. Move on only after it has been mastered.

■ Offer the cat a food treat and extensive praise when it performs the desired behavior.

■ Conduct training sessions at the same time and place every day.

Leash Training

This is not an essential feline function, but it can pay dividends. A cat who is accustomed to a leash will also heed its owner during emergencies. Remember that not all felines are amenable to this. In general, the more "doglike" a cat's behavior, the more accepting it is of leashes.

[1] Purchase a lightweight leash and a harness designed specifically for cats or small dogs. A harness is harder for a cat to wriggle out of than a collar—unless it is too loose. Ideally, you should be able to slip no more than two fingers between the cat and harness.

[2] Allow the cat to adjust to the new pieces of equipment by leaving them near its sleeping area for a few days.

[3] Place the harness on the cat, then immediately tempt the feline with treats or a favorite meal. If it seems uncomfortable or agitated, distract it with play. When the cat seems comfortable with the new arrangement, remove the harness.

[4] Repeat step 3 each day, until the cat is comfortable putting on and wearing the harness.

[5] Attach a leash and let the cat (under your supervision) drag it around the house. Do not attempt to "lead" it. If the feline seems agitated, distract

LEASH PROTOCOL

1. Avoid high-traffic areas
2. Avoid canine models
3. All vaccinations must be current
4. Let the cat lead—never pull it

it with play. Leave the leash and harness on for 15 minutes, then remove them. Repeat daily until the cat is comfortable with the arrangement.

[**6**] Pick up the leash and follow the cat around. Do not pull the leash tight or attempt to lead. Repeat for several days.

[**7**] Take the cat on indoor walks, using a positive, high-pitched voice to get it to follow you. Remember that a cat will not "heel" the way a dog does. It will wander back and forth across the path you select. However, don't allow the cat to cause you to veer from your preselected course. Also, don't aggressively pull the cat to get it to move in your direction. This will only turn the cat against leash training—perhaps forever.

[**8**] Once the feline has mastered indoor leash walking, take it outside— perhaps to a porch or backyard. Allow it several days to grow accustomed to the new environment. Once all nervousness has disappeared, take the cat on experimental walks through quiet, low-stress environments, using the same leash training techniques described above.

EXPERT TIP: It is best to keep walks short and confined to familiar territory. Be wary of encounters with loud vehicles and unescorted dogs.

CAUTION: If you plan to take a housebound cat on leash walks, be sure all vaccinations are up to date, as well as flea and heartworm medications. Also, be sure the feline's rabies and identification tags are attached to its harness.

Sit

[1] Hold a food reward over the cat's head (Fig. A). At the same time, say its name and give the command to "sit."

[2] Move the treat backward over its head until the cat naturally lowers into the sitting position (Fig. B). If it doesn't, lightly press the cat's hindquarters down. Keep the treat above its head and say "sit."

[3] When the cat sits, offer praise and the treat.

[4] Repeat, during daily training sessions, until the feline masters the behavior.

Down

[1] Hold a food reward in front of the cat's face. At the same time, say its name and give the command, "down."

[2] Slowly lower the treat to the cat's chest. Ideally, the cat will lower its body as it follows.

[3] Slowly move the treat away from the cat's face, so that it stretches out to follow it and naturally adopts the "down" position.

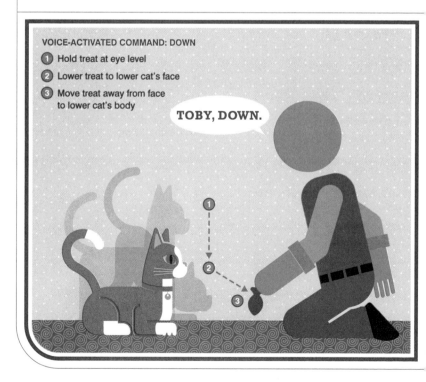

VOICE-ACTIVATED COMMAND: DOWN
1. Hold treat at eye level
2. Lower treat to lower cat's face
3. Move treat away from face to lower cat's body

TOBY, DOWN.

[4] When the cat lies down, offer praise and the treat.

[5] Repeat, during daily training sessions, until the feline masters the be-havior.

⚠ **EXPERT TIP:** *The "sit" and "down" commands can also serve as a modified "stay" behavior. To get the feline to hold these positions longer, gradually lengthen the time between the execution of the behavior and the reward.*

Coming When Called

This behavior can be particularly helpful if your cat ever escapes out-doors.

[1] Pick a spot in the house, sit down, and call to the cat in a pleasant voice. Attract it by any means necessary, including treats.

[2] When the cat comes, offer praise and a reward.

[3] Move to a different location and repeat the exercise.

[4] Repeat over as many days as necessary until the cat reliably comes when called.

⚠ **CAUTION:** *Never call the cat to an unpleasant experience (such as bathing). Instead, go to the cat. Associating unpleasantness with the "come" command will cause the feline to delete the entire subroutine.*

Fetch

Strangely, some cats enjoy this most doglike of games. However, participation is a highly personal choice (for the feline). The only way to know if your cat carries the necessary programming is to try to initiate it.

[1] Toss a small cotton toy in your cat's presence—preferably something the feline particularly enjoys.

[2] Wait until the cat goes to the toy and takes it in its mouth.

[3] Call the cat to you.

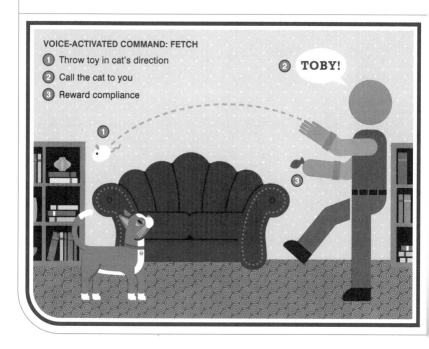

[4] If the cat returns with the toy, offer to trade it for a treat. Praise your cat if it drops the toy in exchange for the treat.

[5] Repeat as many times as necessary until the cat understands what is expected.

Clicker Training

When training a feline, good behavior must be rewarded immediately if the cat is to understand that this is the course it is expected to follow. For instance, an owner who wants to discourage a cat from meowing constantly can do so by rewarding the cat when it is silent—even if that silence lasts for only a few seconds. But in order to do this, the owner must produce a treat the *moment* the desired behavior manifests itself. If he or she hears the cat go silent, then expends five or six seconds looking around for a food reward to offer, the undesirable meowing behavior may resume by the time the reward for the previous, desired behavior is tendered.

One solution is to train the feline to associate a clicker—a metal or plastic handheld "cricket" device that makes a clicking sound—with rewards. This is simple to do. First, click the clicker at dinnertime, just before you put out the cat's food. The feline will rapidly associate the sound with meals and come running when it hears it. Next, make the connection even more obvious using "training" sessions in which you click the clicker once, then provide a treat.

Once the clicker/treat connection is firmly established, employ it during training. If you are teaching the cat to sit, snap the clicker as soon as it adopts the proper position. Then produce a treat. It is important, however, to continue using the appropriate command words ("sit," "stay," etc.) while training the cat.

BUB

CAT SNAX

CHP

E   F

MODEL F-05   *Mixed*

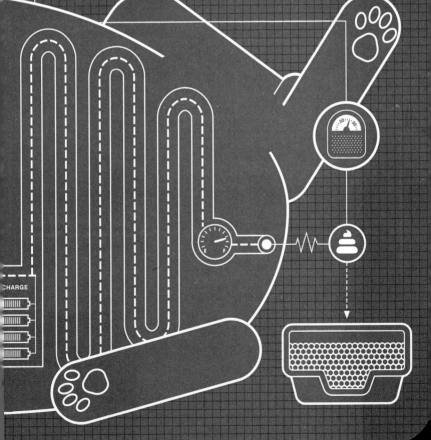

[Chapter 5]

Fuel
Requirements

Types of Fuel

Cat foods are divided into two broad categories—dry and canned. Dry foods contain more calories and nutrition by weight, are less expensive, and may help reduce dental tartar. Canned food is strongly favored by cats themselves, and it includes fewer calories by volume (it is approximately 70 percent water). That extra liquid may help alleviate urinary tract difficulties in older cats. One option is to offer a mix of the two products. Consult your veterinarian for advice.

Special foods are also available to counter everything from hair balls to diabetes to urinary tract dysfunction (which poses a major problem with male cats). When feeding a commercially prepared food, begin by offering your feline the recommended daily serving. Be prepared to adjust this, however, to conform to your feline's specific needs.

Meat

While some carnivores can incorporate a great deal of vegetarian fare into their diets, cats are "pure" predators whose finely tuned physiology requires large quantities of meat and fat to function properly. For instance, cats cannot convert plant-based carotene into vitamin A. They must get this essential element from organ meats. Felines also require a fatty acid found only in animal tissue called arachidonic acid, and they have an unusually high requirement for taurine, an amino acid available only in muscle meats, fish, and shellfish.

This does not mean, however, that felines should eat nothing but meat. Vegetable matter is an important part of all cats' diets. Even exclusively carnivorous models such as lions obtain this material by devouring the stomach contents of their herbivorous prey.

Fuel Facts

■ Cats do well on high-fat diets, which, among other things, aid them in the absorption of vitamins A and E.

■ If extreme circumstances demand it, felines can go for very long periods without food. They can lose as much as 40 percent of their body mass without terminal malfunction.

■ The proportion of fat in a cat's diet should increase as it ages.

■ A cat's protein intake is very high—about 26 percent of a day's calories.

Approximate Daily Fuel Requirements

The typical adult feline requires a daily nutrient total of 1 ounce of canned food or $1/3$ ounce of dry food per pound of body weight. (If your cat's operating system is metric-based, provide approximately 60 grams of canned food or 20 grams of dry food for every kilogram of body weight.) Recommended portions are also listed on the containers of prepackaged foods. Be ready to adjust these, however, if the cat becomes overweight or underweight. (For information on diet requirements for kittens, see page 149.)

Selecting a Brand

Cat food makers are required to post nutritional information about their products on their containers. Such labels must list, among other things, the ingredients and a statement of nutritional purpose and adequacy (essentially, an explanation as to what sort of cat the food is meant for).

Examine the statement of nutritional purpose and adequacy first. A product for kittens might say it offers "complete and balanced nutrition for early development." Or a food for full-grown cats might say, "com-

TYPES OF FUEL: There are two broad categories of fuel: dry and canned

DRY FUEL (front view)

PREMIUM QUALITY

②

①

ADULT CAT FOOD

KITTY KRUNCH

CHICKEN with RICE

GREAT SAVORY MEATY TASTE!

YOUR CAT WILL LOVE IT!

Examine the nutritional purpose and ingredients carefully before selecting a brand.

DRY FUEL (side view)

CANNED FUEL (front view)

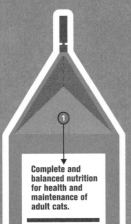

1 Complete and balanced nutrition for health and maintenance of adult cats.

2 Based on AAFCO feeding protocols

Ingredients: Chicken, Chicken Broth, Rice, Wheat Grass Powder, Soy, Carrots, Broccoli, Cabbage, Peas, Ground Flax, Poultry Feathers, Vitamin A Supplement, Niacin Supplement, and Vitamin B12 Supplement **3** **4** **5**

2 PREMIUM QUALITY

KITTY DeLITE with REAL TUNA

DIET CAT FOOD **1**

1 Complete and balanced nutrition for health and maintenance of overweight cats

2 Based on AAFCO feeding protocols

Ingredients: Tuna, Lamb Broth, Liver, Wheat Grass Powder, Soy, Broccoli, Peas, Bonemeal, Vitamin A Supplement, and Niacin Supplement **3** **4** **5**

CANNED FUEL (back view)

1 Nutritional purpose and adequacy statement

2 Indicates a high-quality product that was subjected to a feeding study.

The order in which the ingredients are listed is determined by weight (heaviest is listed first)

3 Meat should be near the top of the list

4 Cereals and soy should be listed prominently

5 Vitamins, minerals, and preservatives should appear last, as they are used minutely

plete nutrition to support the health of adult cats." The best products will state that they are "Formulated to meet the AAFCO (Association of American Feed Control Officials) Cat Food Nutrient Profile for . . ." Do not buy pet foods that do not mention the AAFCO on their labels.

After selecting a balanced, nutritionally complete product fine-tuned to your cat's needs, examine the ingredients. The heaviest by weight is listed first. Wet foods almost always list a meat product first, while in dry preparations meat may appear farther down the roster. This is because in wet foods the meat is hydrated and therefore heavier. Dry products may contain just as much meat, but because it weighs less it sits slightly lower on the ingredient list. In general, one or even two meat products should be at or near the top of the list. Meat by-products (these can range from bonemeal to fish skin) are generally of lower quality.

Also study the "guaranteed analysis" section of the label, which among other things states what percentage of the food is composed of such important elements as crude protein, crude fat, and crude fiber (an adult feline–maintenance food should ideally contain a *minimum* of 26 percent protein and 9 percent fat; a formulation for kittens and pregnant or lactating females should contain no less than 30 percent protein).

It is also vital to examine the wording on the front of the label. If a product advertises itself as "chicken cat food," then at least 95 percent of the product must be composed of the named item (or 70 percent, if moisture content is included). If the product contains more than 25 percent but less than 95 percent of its signature item, then it must be called "chicken formula," "chicken platter," or use some other qualifier. And foods incorporating the word "with" (as in "cat food with chicken") may include as little as 3 percent of the named ingredient.

How to Feed

In general, it is inadvisable to "free feed"—that is, to leave a bowl of food sitting out all day so the feline can serve itself. While younger cats tend to regulate their intake, overeating and obesity become greater concerns as the feline ages and its activity level declines. Also, in multicat households it is difficult to determine which unit consumes how much.

The best approach is to select a standard time to offer a meal (it should not vary from day to day), then present the food. In most cases there will be no question of leftovers; once the cat understands the system, it will polish off each portion rapidly. Two meals a day, one in the morning and one in the evening (to correspond to the feline's traditional hunting times), are sufficient for an adult cat. Make sure, however, that its total portion does not exceed the unit's recommended daily caloric intake.

Very young kittens can have as much food as they care to consume, usually provided in three- or four-times-a-day feedings. As the kitten ages, gradually decrease the frequency of feedings. A 6-month-old cat should be ready for the standard two-a-day regimen.

EXPERT TIP: *Feeding the cat during family mealtimes may prevent the feline from milling around the table, begging for scraps.*

Water Intake

Fresh, clean water should be available at all times. In general, a cat will take in twice as much water as dry food. A feline who eats wet food (which is composed of 75 percent water or more) will derive most of its daily water intake from its meal and may drink sparingly, if at all.

FUEL SUPPLEMENTS

NUTRITIOUS SNACKS

1. Low-calorie cat treats
2. Tidbits of cooked green beans or carrots
3. Indoor grass
4. Cooked pasta or rice
5. Dollop of yogurt

HAZARDOUS MATERIALS

1. Dog food
2. Onions
3. Table scraps
4. Milk
5. Macadamia nuts
6. Tea, coffee, or other caffeinated beverages

Fuel Supplements (Snacks)

Snacks should comprise no more than 10 percent of a cat's daily caloric intake. Appropriate snacks include:

- Commercial, low-calorie cat treats
- Cooked vegetable tidbits, such as carrots and green beans
- Grass grown indoors in a pot. Cats occasionally like to "graze."
- A small amount of cooked pasta or rice
- A dollop of yogurt

The following consumables are unhealthy and possibly fatal to cats:

- Dog food (It is not formulated to meet feline needs.)
- Onions (Too much can trigger anemia.)
- Table scraps (These can cause obesity and stomach upset.)
- Milk (Many cats, like many adult mammals, are lactose intolerant. Milk can cause stomach upset and diarrhea.)
- Macadamia nuts (An unknown toxin in them makes felines very ill.)
- Tea, coffee, or any other beverage or food containing high amounts of caffeine (which is extremely dangerous for cats)

Fueling Glitches

Any number of factors can cause a cat to lose interest in its food. Some of the most common include a sudden change of diet; boredom with monotonous fare; a change of season (felines often eat less in summer than in winter); stress; intimidation by another cat, a dog, or a child; even location of the food bowl in an inappropriately busy spot. Often, solving the problem is as simple as varying the diet slightly—providing an occasional dose of wet food to go with dry, or even raising the temperature of the meal. Felines, who as predators dined on fresh kills,

prefer their food warm—or at least at room temperature. Thus a cat may accept wet food from a freshly opened (unrefrigerated) can, but turn up its nose at cold leftovers that have been stored in the refrigerator.

⚠ *CAUTION: If a normally hungry cat suddenly stops eating, monitor the situation carefully. If it persists for more than 24 hours, contact your veterinarian. Loss of appetite can signal malfunction.*

Managing a Cat's Weight

Stand over the feline and put your fingers on its rib cage. In a normal cat you should be able to feel the individual ribs, covered by a thin layer of fat. In an obese cat, you will not be able to feel them. Next, examine the cat's shape and gait. Obese cats develop a protruding abdomen, along with fatty deposits at the base of the tail, over the hips, and on the neck and chest. Overweight cats also waddle when they walk.

Weighing a Cat

[**1**] Weigh yourself on a bathroom scale (Fig. A).

[**2**] Pick up the cat and weigh again (Fig. B).

[**3**] Subtract the first weight from the second weight (Fig. C).

[**4**] If the cat resists being lifted, cancel the process immediately (Fig. D).

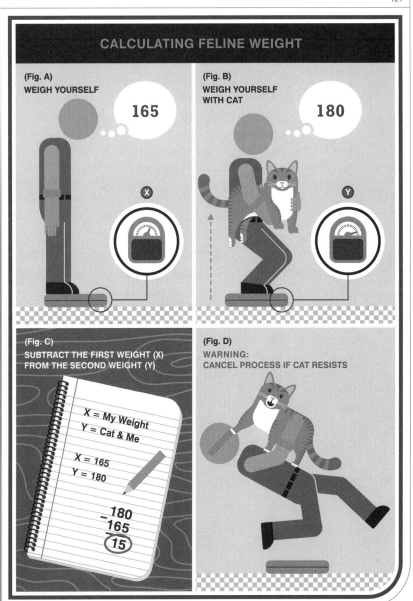

Weight Reduction

Obesity, in most cases, occurs when the cat's caloric intake exceeds its daily requirements for normal maintenance. Roughly one-fourth of domestic cats are overweight. As in humans, this can lead to malfunctions such as arthritis, heart disease, and liver problems. Keeping your feline close to its ideal weight is essential if it is to lead a long and healthy life.

Before changing your cat's diet, develop a plan of action with your veterinarian. Weight loss in felines takes time and is not without risks. In some cases, a special diet may be needed, or there may be other complicating factors to consider. Feline obesity can also lead to diabetes.

Keep the following tips in mind as you proceed with your program:

■ Caloric intake is lowered either by decreasing the ration of the cat's current food or by placing the feline on a low-calorie product. *This should only be done under a veterinarian's supervision.*

■ Make sure the cat has plenty of water, as this may help it to feel full.

■ "Bulking up" a cat's meals with low- or no-calorie fiber additives will help it feel satiated.

■ If your veterinarian approves, increase the cat's level of physical activity. Additional playtime will usually suffice.

■ All family members must agree to adhere to the feline's new diet plan. A single family member providing unauthorized treats can derail the effort.

■ Food portions must be measured exactly to make sure the recommended portion is not exceeded.

■ If you have multiple cats, feed them in separate locations so the dieting cat does not receive extra food. Do not leave food for the other felines sitting out unsupervised.

- Avoid fatty snacks. Reward the cat with low-calorie treats such as air-popped popcorn, green beans, or carrots.
- Follow-up visits, on whatever schedule your veterinarian thinks appropriate, are necessary to monitor weight loss.
- Most dieting felines require 8 to 12 months to reach their target weight.
- The maximum weight a cat can safely lose in 1 week is $1/8$ to $1/4$ pound (112–225 g).

Underweight Cats

Because felines are sometimes finicky eaters who may refuse their food for any number of reasons, this is a bigger problem than most might assume. A cat is underweight if you can not only feel its ribs distinctly but see them, too. Thin cats also have abnormally narrow waists, protruding rib cages, and visible shoulder blades and spines. If you feel your cat is underweight, contact your veterinarian immediately. Aside from insufficient fuel, a number of physical problems (including cancer, kidney disease, and hyperthyroidism) can trigger this phenomenon.

Modifying Diet

Suddenly changing a cat's diet can lead to stomach upset or to refusal of the new food. To avoid this, switch products gradually. On the first day, offer one-fourth new food and three-fourths old food. On the second day, offer equal portions. After a few days, offer three-fourths new and one-fourth old. Then switch entirely to the new food.

MODEL F-06 *Himalayan*

[Chapter 6]

Exterior Maintenance

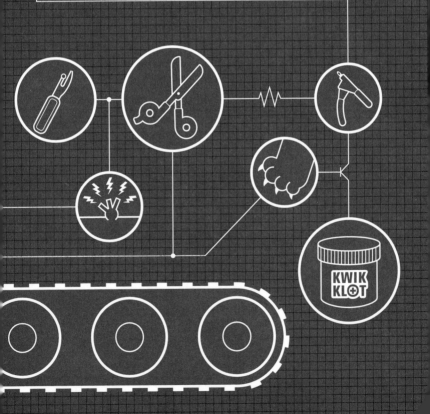

The amount of exterior detailing required by cats varies from model to model. For instance, while shorthaired varieties are relatively easy to maintain, those with longer coats (Persians, Himalayans, Maine Coons) require much more extensive owner (and, sometimes, professional) intervention. However, many non-coat issues, from nail upkeep to bathing protocols, are the same regardless of breed. Whatever your model, regular exterior maintenance will ensure that your feline remains in top operating condition.

Understanding the Coat

Most cat coats include three types of hair. Long, coarse "guard hairs" form the outer coat, while the denser inner coat is composed of medium-length "awn hairs" and soft, short "down hairs." Feline whiskers, also called *vibrissae*, are an additional, extremely specialized hair type.

Not all cats utilize the three main types of coat hairs in the same proportion. For instance, the Angora has very long guard hairs and down hairs, but no awn hairs. Cats use their fur not just as protection from cold and heat, but also to signal their moods and as a defensive measure. For instance, if a cat is in a confrontation and wants to make itself look more intimidating, it will cause its tail and back hairs to stand erect, creating the illusion of added bulk.

While the composition of feline coats varies from model to model, they can be divided into two broad categories: shorthaired and longhaired. Short coats are by far the more common of the two, since the genes for this option are dominant over those for long hair. (In the wild, a low-maintenance short coat makes more sense than a long one.)

Feline shedding is largely a seasonal event. Its intensity increases as the days become longer and winter turns to spring. Indoor cats tend to shed smaller amounts, but do so year-round. Stress and illness can trigger excessive shedding, and a female who has just had kittens may also shed more than usual.

General Coat Maintenance

Regular grooming minimizes hair deposits in your home, makes your cat more attractive, and can lessen or even prevent the problem of hairball regurgitation. (See "Hair Balls," page 142.) Most cats will accept, even welcome, assistance with coat maintenance. In the feline world, reciprocal grooming is a way to build relationships and an opportunity for relaxation. To ensure that the cat views coat maintenance in this way, begin rudimentary grooming during kittenhood, to acclimate the young feline to the procedure.

EXPERT TIP: *Grooming is an ideal time to examine your cat for irritated skin, lumps, bumps, ticks, fleas, and any other problem that might require veterinary attention.*

Grooming Tools

The following accessories will aid in the maintenance of the cat's exterior finish.

Brush: The ideal tool is a soft wire or bristle brush that can remove tangles without irritating skin.

Comb: Usually made of steel and featuring both fine and coarse teeth, this tool can bring order to the coat of a longhaired cat.

Currycomb: Often made of rubber, this tool removes loose hair from short-haired models.

Grooming Glove: Covered with nubby, hair-catching material, the glove is useful for face grooming, and for cats that will not tolerate brushes.

Nail Clippers: Purchase a set specifically designed for cats.

Scissors: Excellent for removing particularly stubborn tangles.

Seam Ripper: A sewing accessory that is also very useful for untangling mats.

Styptic Powder: This blood-clotting powder (available at most commercial retailers) will quickly stop bleeding caused by trimming a cat's nails too closely.

Toothbrush: Useful for grooming the faces of longhaired cats and for dental hygiene on all models. (Use separate brushes for these functions.)

Chamois Cloth: Imparts a glossy finish to the exterior of shorthaired models.

Selecting a Professional Groomer

Most owners can easily handle the grooming needs of a shorthaired cat. However, longhaired varieties may require regular professional intervention. Most veterinarians keep lists of recommended groomers; a few even employ groomers on staff. Additional sources for recommendations include friends, reputable purebred dealers, and local cat clubs.

If your model has special needs (for instance, if it is geriatric or wary around strangers), make sure your choice is equipped to meet them. Visit the salon during business hours for an unscheduled inspection. Are the facilities clean? Is everything neat and orderly? Are cats segregated from dogs? What you pay will depend on the feline's condition and the complexity of the work.

⚠ *CAUTION: Before taking your cat to a groomer, make sure your pet's vaccinations are current.*

Grooming Techniques

Methods and approaches vary for longhaired and shorthaired cats.

For Longhairs

Many longhaired breeds require 15 to 30 minutes of daily attention. Otherwise, they develop painful mats in their coats. (See "Removing Mats," page 131.)

[1] Use the wide-tooth side of a double-sided comb to clear tangles. Once this is accomplished, switch to the fine-tooth comb and repeat.

[2] Use a wire brush to remove dead hair. The feline's posterior quadrant will yield the most abundant supply.

[3] Run the fine-tooth comb through the hair in an upward direction (from the tail toward the head) to increase the coat's volume.

GROOMING PROTOCOL

↑ LONGHAIR MODEL

↓ SHORTHAIR MODEL

1 Wire Brush 2 Fine-tooth Comb 3 Wide-tooth Comb 4 Toothbrush

5 Bristle Brush 6 Currycomb 7 Double-sided Comb 8 Chamois Cloth

[4] Use a toothbrush to groom facial hair. Do not use the brush near the eyes.

[5] Repeat step 3 with the wide-tooth comb, in order to help the hair stand up.

For Shorthairs

These models require perhaps two grooming sessions per week.

[1] Comb from head to tail with a fine-tooth metal comb.

[2] Repeat this process using a rubber currycomb or soft natural-bristle brush.

[3] To bring the coat to a high shine, rub a chamois cloth over its surface.

Removing Mats

Mats are created when dead hair deep in the coat becomes entangled with fast-growing new hair. They usually form very close to the skin and can be quite painful. To disentangle one, first (if possible) place a comb between the mat and the feline's skin, to serve as a barrier against accidental cuts. Then use a seam ripper on the outside of the matted material, working your way toward the center as the hair loosens. If the mat cannot be entirely removed, cut out the remainder with scissors (placing a comb between the hair and the cat's skin will protect the animal from accidental cuts and nicks).

⚠️ **CAUTION:** *In cases of severe matting, the cat may have to be partially or completely shaved. This procedure should be performed by a competent groomer. If your cat aggressively resists grooming, a veterinarian may need to remove the matting after placing the cat under anesthesia.*

Bathing

While some cats will rarely, if ever, require a bath, others, including longhaired models and elderly, ill, or disabled felines, may need help in maintaining themselves. Be sure to use a shampoo and conditioner specially formulated for cats; products intended for humans are too harsh for felines.

[**1**] Place a rubber mat in a large sink. The mat will give the cat a secure footing on which to stand. (See Fig. A, p. 134.)

[**2**] Gather your supplies (see Fig. B, p. 134). Brush the cat's coat before bathing to remove any dead hair and to locate (and remove) any tangles.

[**3**] Apply a drop of mineral oil to the corner of each eye, to keep out soap (see Fig. C, p. 134).

[**4**] Fill the sink with warm water; 101.4°F (38.5°C), the standard feline body temperature, is ideal.

[**5**] Holding the cat firmly, submerge it in the sink up to its shoulders, until the coat is completely soaked. Reassure the feline. If the cat becomes extremely agitated and/or panics, discontinue procedure immediately.

[**6**] Drain sink. Using a wet cloth, apply a small amount of the shampoo to the cat's face, scrupulously avoiding the eyes, ears, and mouth. Then remove using another wet cloth. Do not pour or spray water on the cat's head.

[**7**] With the sink still drained, apply special cat-formulated shampoo to the feline's body (see Fig. D, p. 135). Gently work it in. Remember the tail and waste elimination port.

[**8**] Refill the sink with tepid water and rinse. It may take several sink refills to achieve full shampoo removal (see Fig. E, p. 135). Some cats may tolerate a spray nozzle or being positioned under the tap. However, do not pour or spray water on the feline's head. Note: If effective shampoo removal is a problem, mix $1/2$ cup (118 ml) vinegar with 2 quarts (1.8 l) water, then ladle this over the cat's body. This will strip any remaining soap residue. Be sure to rinse with clean water after this application.

[**9**] Blot fur dry, then place the feline on the floor or a counter. Shorthaired cats need only a vigorous toweling, followed by some time in a warm room. Longhaired cats require a thorough combing and, perhaps, a blow-dry (see Fig. F, p. 135).

EXPERT TIP: When employing a blow-dryer, always use the lowest heat setting. Begin with the torso by aiming the nozzle against the lay of the hair. Then move to the legs and neck. To avoid curl, make sure each section is totally dry. Save the tail, stomach, and back legs for last, because contact with these areas can upset felines. Discontinue if the cat becomes agitated.

 CAUTION: Keep the cat in a warm place until its hair is completely dry.

(Fig. A)
INSTALL RUBBER MAT

(Fig. B)
GATHER SUPPLIES

1. Shampoo
2. Ladle
3. Washcloth
4. Mineral oil
5. Comb
6. Towel or blow-dryer

KITTY KLEEN
IT'S JUST... PURRRFECT!

(Fig. C)
FELINE PREPARATION

101.4°F (38.5°C)

BATHING PROCEDURE: While some models can maintain themselves,

(Fig. D)
APPLY CAT-FORMULATED SHAMPOO

(Fig. E)
GENTLY RINSE OFF SHAMPOO

(Fig. F)
DRY THOROUGHLY

LOW

longhaired or physically disabled felines may need to be bathed manually.

Nails

The nails of indoor cats may occasionally grow too long, in which case clipping is required. (This procedure can also minimize danger to your household furnishings.) Here is the appropriate method.

[1] Purchase a set of trimmers specifically designed for cats.

[2] Hold cat firmly on your lap, or enlist an assistant to hold it.

[3] Squeeze the front of the paw. The nails should automatically deploy.

[4] Nip off the sharp point. This is usually sufficient for most felines. Avoid the "quick"—the pinkish area farther down the nail that carries nerve endings and the blood supply. If you accidentally cut this area, stop the bleeding by applying styptic powder (a commercially available blood-clotting compound).

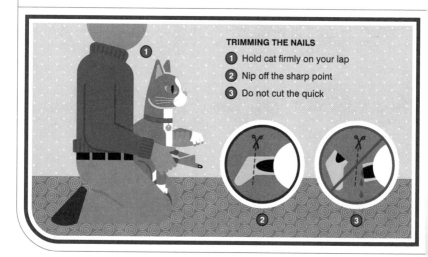

TRIMMING THE NAILS
1. Hold cat firmly on your lap
2. Nip off the sharp point
3. Do not cut the quick

Declawing

Because the cat's off-the-shelf design is so elegant, owners have rarely been tempted to make postnatal changes. One exception is the procedure known as declawing, or onychectomy. Usually done to prevent destructive scratching of home furnishings, the operation removes the claws on the forepaws using a technique comparable to the removal of human fingertips at the top knuckle. The procedure can sometimes cause severe, lasting pain for adult cats. Though common in the United States, this modification is against the law in Germany, England, and Switzerland, where it is considered animal cruelty. This procedure should be contemplated only if other methods of stopping excessive clawing (regular nail clipping, behavior modification, and/or placing "caps" on the claws) have failed, and the choice is between performing the procedure or surrendering the cat to a shelter.

Ears

The ears should be checked regularly for signs of unpleasant odor, redness, and/or inflammation, all of which should be examined by a veterinarian. Professional service is also required if a cat is constantly scratching its ears. To clean the ears, use a cotton ball moistened with water. Clean only the external, visible portion; do not probe the ear canal. Do not use a cotton swab, except under a veterinarian's advice.

Eyes

A healthy cat's eyes should always be shiny and free of discoloration. Some models may have long facial hairs that get into the eyes and cause irritation and/or corneal damage. Watch for this problem, and make sure your groomer keeps the cat's face clear. Do not attempt to cut the long facial hairs yourself, because you might poke the cat in the eye with the scissors. Examine the eyes for discharge, and wipe away deposits with a warm cloth or with a commercial tear-stain-removal product. If the problem (particularly common with Persians and Himalayans) persists, or if the discharge is discolored or excessive, consult your veterinarian.

Teeth

Cats are prone to plaque buildup and gingivitis. This common feline ailment can be detected in its early stages by a home dental inspection. Examine the teeth for discoloration, tartar buildup, chipped or missing teeth, and signs of wear. Also examine the gums for signs of inflammation or discoloration. Remember that an oral infection can be very dangerous. A long-term problem can become a drain on the cat's internal organs and/or immune system—not to mention the fact that the infection is located just inches from the feline's central processing unit. Regularly brushing your cat's teeth, while somewhat difficult, can help head off dental problems.

 EXPERT TIP: *A diet of hard food can also reduce plaque.*

Brushing Your Cat's Teeth

This procedure is usually much easier if the cat is accustomed to it as a kitten. If this is not the case, your feline may have to become habituated to the process. During play or grooming sessions, when the cat is relaxed and happy, make a point of briefly rubbing its muzzle. When it becomes comfortable with this, gently handle its teeth and gums. Only when the cat becomes accustomed to these invasions is it fruitful to attempt brushing. Most veterinarians recommend that you brush a cat's teeth two to three times a week.

[1] Procure a soft-bristle toothbrush (this is the only such device that gets below the gum line) and a toothpaste specially formulated for cats. The human variety (especially those containing baking soda) can cause indigestion.

[2] Offer the cat a taste of the toothpaste. Most are specially designed to be highly palatable and flavorful. Repeat this procedure daily until the feline is comfortable with the process.

[3] Rub the toothpaste along the gums of the upper teeth. Repeat this procedure daily until the feline is comfortable with the process.

[4] Use the toothbrush. Focus on the gum line. Work from back to front. It should take approximately 30 seconds to do the entire mouth.

Do not try to brush the entire mouth the first time. Gradually build up brushing time until you can cover all the teeth in the allotted half-minute.

EXPERT TIP: Brushing before a meal or a regular treat will help your cat see dental maintenance as a positive experience.

Emergency Cleanups

Whenever you locate foreign or unidentified substances on your cat's coat, it is best to remove them immediately. Otherwise, the cat may ingest them via licking, which may lead to malfunction.

Burrs: Most can be removed with careful use of a metal comb. Deeply entangled burrs can often be released by working vegetable oil into the affected area. If this method fails to work, carefully remove the burrs with scissors.

Chewing Gum: Apply ice to the gum to reduce its stickiness, then clip from fur. Alternatively, there are several commercial products that facilitate gum removal without haircutting.

Paint: If it is a water-based paint, soak the affected area in water for 5 minutes or longer until it becomes pliant. Then rub the affected fur between your fingers to remove it. Any other type of paint will require careful clipping and trimming.

⚠ *CAUTION: Never use paint thinner, turpentine, gasoline, or any other such solvents on your cat.*

Skunk: If your cat is sprayed by a skunk, you can de-scent it with a thorough bath in tomato juice. Hold the cat in a basin filled with tomato juice; allow the exterior coat to soak in the juice for several minutes, then rinse and repeat. The cat may require several baths (over several days) before the scent disappears.

Tar: In many cases the tar-coated hair will have to be clipped away. However, petroleum jelly can sometimes remove the substance. Rub some into a small portion of the affected area, then wipe away the broken-up tar with a clean cloth. Repeat as many times as necessary. Bathe the cat with a degreasing shampoo afterward.

Controlling Cat-Hair Deposits in the Home

Loose cat hair adhering to furnishings and floating through the air is more than just an aesthetic problem. Because it is usually coated with a powerful allergen present in cat saliva (and deposited on the coat during self-grooming), it can also trigger allergies and asthma. The best way to minimize the impact of feline shedding is to stop it at its source, by regularly grooming your cat. If rogue hair continues to be a problem, here are some ways to control it.

■ Professional groomers offer regimens that combine special baths and extensive brushing to curtail heavy shedding for several weeks.

■ Devices called corner combs can be attached to the corners of walls. Placed at cat height, they are essentially bristled combs that felines enjoy rubbing against, extracting loose hair in the process.

■ If your cat favors a particular chair or section of the couch, place a piece of fabric on that spot for the feline to lie on. Never wash the fabric with other clothes, which will pick up the hair.

■ Wash hair-infested clothes with multiple dryer sheets—the better to help the hair make its way to the lint trap.

- Particularly stubborn deposits can be removed from rugs, carpets, and upholstery by using a damp towel, which bunches up the hair into easily removable balls.
- Fabric sprays that negate static cling also repel cat hair.
- Fabric softener sheets can be rubbed over clothing to pick up cat hair.

Hair Balls

During grooming, cats may ingest a great deal of their own loose hair. Normally this passes through their bodies and is downloaded as a waste product. But if a feline takes in too much hair too quickly, the mass may be regurgitated as a hair ball. Longhaired cats tend to suffer the most from this problem simply because they have the most hair. However, all felines may eject fur balls from time to time. The best way to avoid (or minimize) this unsightly problem is to carefully groom the cat. The more dead hair that is brushed away, the less there is for the feline to ingest. A number of petroleum-based products are also available in pastes or treats that act as a mild laxative, helping the hair pass through the cat's system.

⚠️ *CAUTION: If your cat attempts repeatedly and unsuccessfully to pass a fur ball (and also displays constipation and loss of appetite), the mass may be lodged in the stomach or small intestine. This is a potentially life-threatening malfunction. Consult your veterinarian immediately.*

⚠ WARNING: All models will periodically eject hair balls.

HAIR BALLS:

1. Formed from hair ingested while grooming
2. May be relieved by specially formulated products
3. May be prevented with careful grooming
4. May be passed as waste . . .
5. . . . or regurgitated

HAIR-B-GONE

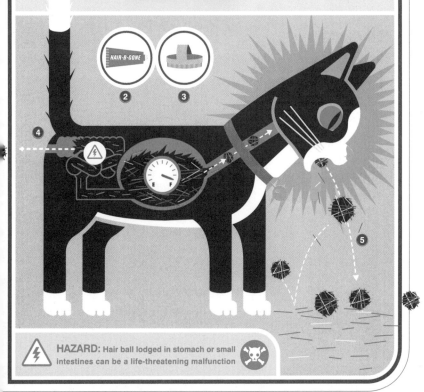

⚠ HAZARD: Hair ball lodged in stomach or small intestines can be a life-threatening malfunction ☠

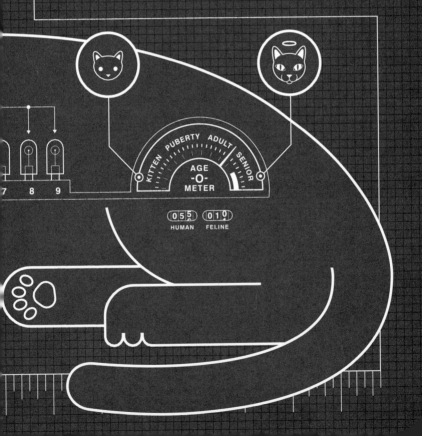

[Chapter 7]

Growth and Development

Kitten Growth Stages

The feline includes many unique features that are either rare or unavailable in the vast majority of consumer products. While most such devices can only be upgraded by purchasing and installing expensive peripherals, the cat has the ability to increase its cognitive and mechanical capacities on its own. This phenomenon is most obvious in kittens, who in a matter of weeks upgrade from helpless, highly dependent units into fully mature systems. This section offers an overview of that remarkable process.

Birth to 8 Weeks

About two-thirds of kittens are born headfirst, and about one-third tail first. They are born blind, deaf, unable to walk, and weighing only about 4 ounces (113 g). Eyelids open at 10 to 12 days of age. Ears open at 14 to 17 days. Kittens begin to crawl at 16 to 20 days, to walk at 22 to 25 days, and to run at 4 to 5 weeks. Consumption of solid food begins at 3 to 4 weeks.

Programming Milestones: Litter box training will begin at 3 to 4 weeks. Under normal circumstances this will be taught by the kitten's mother. The owner's only responsibility is to provide clean, easily accessible litter pans and to watch to make sure the training "takes." Kittens will begin to clean themselves at 4 to 5 weeks, play with littermates at 4 to 5 weeks, and practice hunting techniques at 6 to 8 weeks. Most of these downloads will occur without human input.

This is also a crucial time for socialization. Frequent, gentle handling beginning at 14 days helps a very young kitten become accustomed to people. However, the kitten should remain with its mother and littermates during these weeks. Only they can help it download essential feline programming.

⚠ *CAUTION: A feline mother will occasionally carry her kittens by the scruff of the neck. Do not emulate this behavior, as it may cause injury to the kitten.*

8 to 15 Weeks

Full weaning takes place at or before 8 weeks. Kittens can be supplied with small amounts of thinned gruel (dry food mixed with water) as early as their third or fourth week. As time passes, the amount of liquid in the meal can be reduced and the solid matter increased. All baby or "milk" teeth are present at 8 weeks. Males begin to outweigh females at approximately 10 weeks of age. At 12 weeks, eye color (which in very young kittens is almost always blue) changes to permanent adult hue. The first physical exam, stool check, and immunization should occur at 9 weeks. Kittens may leave their mother for a new home anywhere from the age of 8 to 10 weeks, depending on when it makes the transition to solid food. This transition should occur automatically without human input.

Programming Milestones: Sibling interaction during play teaches kittens the importance of retracting their claws and not inflicting serious bites.

⚠ *CAUTION: Do not take unvaccinated kittens outdoors, unless it is for a trip to the veterinarian.*

15 Weeks to Adulthood

Permanent, "adult" teeth appear between 12 and 18 weeks. Spaying of females can take place as early as 16 weeks. Males can be neutered as early as 16 weeks. While female cats reach their adult weight at roughly 12 months of age, males keep growing until about 15 months.

Programming Milestones: Total independence from mother (if the kitten has not already been adopted by a human family) occurs at 6 months.

Calculating Age in "Cat Years"

A popular misconception is that cats age seven years for each calendar year. In fact, feline aging is much more rapid during the first two years of life. A cat reaches the approximate human age of 15 during its first year, then 24 at age 2. Each year thereafter, it ages approximately four "cat years" for every calendar year. Thus, a 5-year-old feline would be approximately 36 in cat years. It should be remembered that a cat who lives outdoors ages far more quickly, perhaps even twice as fast, than an indoor cat.

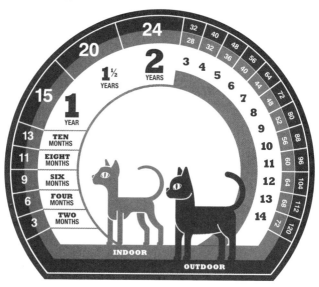

Diet Requirements

Kittens demand tremendous amounts of energy. Once weaned, they should receive a high-quality food tailored to their needs. Such products contain roughly 35 percent protein, 12 to 24 percent fat, and about one-fourth more calories than fuel that is formulated for adults. The food should be provided several times a day, or left in the kitten enclosure so the felines can "free feed" (there is little chance that kittens will become obese). Supplemental "wet" food can also be provided once or twice a day.

Kittens who sample several different products may grow up to be less finicky eaters; however, too much variety may cause stomach upset. Continue feeding kitten food until the feline is 9 months old or has reached 80 to 90 percent of its probable adult weight (consult your veterinarian). Then gradually switch to an adult-formulated product. (See "Modifying Diet," page 123.) Do not give vitamins or other supplements to kittens without consulting your veterinarian. Be sure the kitten has access to fresh water throughout the day.

⚠️ *CAUTION: Because kittens' nutritional needs are very exact, developing a regimen of homemade food is in most cases not practical. Even minor imbalances can have devastating consequences. For instance, a taurine deficiency can cause blindness.*

Sexual Maturity

In general, males reach sexual maturity at 10 to 14 months; females at 7 to 12 months. Unaltered females typically go into heat (estrus) three or more times a year. During this period the female is receptive to the advances of males and capable of breeding. She may signal her readiness with loud, insistent calling, though some females do not call at all.

Instead, they may simply become more friendly and solicit more attention from their owners. Keep the female confined or under close observation during these times, because she will attract every intact male in the area. Do not leave the female alone in such semi-secure spots as screened porches; this often isn't enough to stop a determined male.

Male cats have no "cycle." They can breed year-round and will act whenever they encounter a receptive female. Male sexual maturity will also manifest itself in constant roaming and in the marking of territory with urine. (See "Spaying and Neutering," below.)

Spaying and Neutering

It is the duty of every responsible pet owner to have his or her feline spayed or neutered. Unwanted litters contribute to a vast oversupply of cats in the United States. This is a particular problem because felines, if left unchecked, can reproduce in staggering numbers over a short period.

Unless you plan to breed your cat (which is not recommended, except in the case of highly valued purebred models), it should be sterilized before reaching sexual maturity. For males this is called *neutering* (removal of the testicles); for females, *spaying* (removal of the ovaries and uterus). Without neutering, the habits of a male cat (marking its territory with urine; engaging in fights with other males; patrolling ceaselessly in search of females in heat) can be nearly intolerable. The neutering process deletes these subroutines along with the testicles. Neutered males also experience fewer health problems.

Likewise, female cats spayed before puberty are spared such malfunctions as uterine and ovarian cancer—two common disorders. Female cats will also stop going into heat (a two-week-long trial of house-soiling and howling that occurs three or more times each year).

ADVANTAGES OF SPAYING AND NEUTERING

NEUTERING THE MALE REDUCES THE RISK OF:

1 Territorial urination

2 Fighting other males

3 Patrolling for females

SPAYING THE FEMALE REDUCES THE RISK OF:

4 House soiling

5 Howling

6 Unwanted kittens

7 Uterine cancer

8 Ovarian cancer

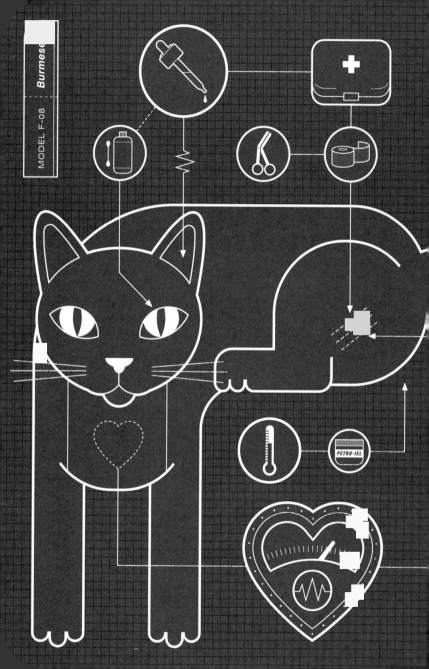

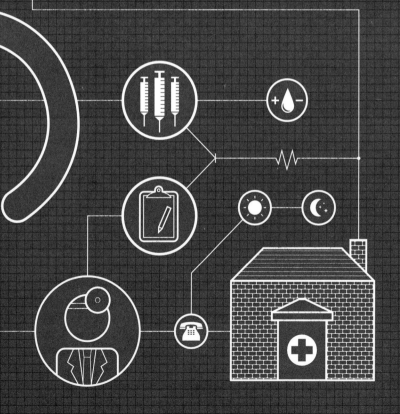

Chapter 8

Interior
Maintenance

Cat owners can call on a vast and highly developed service and support infrastructure for assistance with mechanical or software glitches. This chapter explains how to locate and properly utilize a qualified service provider in your area.

Selecting a Service Provider

One of the first and most important tasks a new cat owner must accomplish is selecting the right veterinarian. The ideal candidate will be available to service your pet over its entire life span. He or she can maintain long-term treatment and immunization records; chart reactions to specific medications; even develop an understanding of your cat's particular programming quirks. This extensive knowledge base will be helpful during minor emergencies and can mean the difference between life and death during major ones. Here are some guidelines to consider when selecting a service provider.

■ When developing a list of candidates, consult fellow cat owners. Cat clubs can also provide lists of recommended vets, including, in some cases, veterinarians with special knowledge of particular models.

■ Schedule an appointment with the veterinarians you are considering. Discuss your cat's specific needs. Be sure you feel comfortable with the vet.

■ Examine the facility. Does it look and smell clean? What range of services and diagnostic equipment does it provide? How are emergency after-hours calls handled?

■ Make sure your choice is a good logistical fit. Does the clinic keep business hours that are convenient for you? Is the office conveniently located? Patronizing a vet with odd hours and an out-of-the-way location is difficult at best, life-threatening at worst.

■ Consider using a "cats only" veterinary practice. Though comparatively small in number, they offer unique advantages. They are generally quieter, the staff is completely focused on feline problems, and there are no dogs present.

⚠ **EXPERT TIP:** *You might want to select a veterinarian before acquiring a cat. If you are unsure about what model to choose or where to acquire one, a veterinarian can provide expert advice.*

Conducting a Home Maintenance Inspection

Cat owners should inspect their models regularly for potential health problems. The best time to do this is during the feline's regular grooming regimen. Here are some systems to review.

Mouth: Teeth should be white, with no cracks, discoloration, or tartar deposits. Gums, tongue, and the insides of the cheeks should be uniformly pink, with no swelling or irritation. The cat's breath, though perhaps slightly "fishy," should not be noxious.

Nose: There should be no discharge or ragged, congested breathing. Constant sneezing is a sign of possible malfunction.

Eyes: A healthy cat should have clear eyes that don't bulge or appear cloudy, red, or irritated. The third eyelid should be barely visible in each interior corner. A prominent third eyelid is a sign of illness.

Output Port: Be sure this area is clean, dry, and free of bumps and welts.

HOME MAINTENANCE INSPECTION

HEALTHY MODEL

1. Clean white teeth, pink gums (unless naturally pigmented black)
2. Clear eyes
3. Pink inside, no discharge
4. Even, shiny coat without flea dirt or skin irritations
5. Clean waste port
6. Clean paws
7. Proper weight

UNHEALTHY MODEL

1. Discharge, tenderness, itching
2. Discharge, squinting, irritation, or cloudiness
3. Noxious breath
4. Dirty waste port
5. Bald spots
6. Flea dirt
7. Excessive shedding
8. Overweight or underweight
9. Cracked paws

Ears: The interiors should be clean, odorless, and free of dark-colored discharge. There should be no tenderness, pain, or itching. The cat should not continually scratch its ears or shake its head.

Weight: If you cannot feel the cat's ribs, the unit may be overweight. If the ribs are very pronounced, the feline could be underweight. Be advised that the gain or loss of a half pound in a week is reason for a veterinary consultation.

Paws: Check condition of claws (if present), and make sure the pads are clean, without cracks, and otherwise in good condition.

Skin: Run your fingers over the cat's body. Check for irritated spots, bumps, or places where the feline reacts negatively when touched. Also, use a comb to examine the skin for "flea dirt" (excrement from fleas that resembles grains of pepper). Skin should be free of odor, grease, scabs, flakes, and other irritations.

Coat: Check for bald spots, dullness, and/or excessive, unwarranted shedding. Contact your veterinarian if your cat stops grooming entirely, as this is often a sign of malfunction.

EXPERT TIP: Felines are programmed to conceal pain and discomfort, so getting an accurate reading on their health can often be difficult. For this reason it is important to carefully observe your cat's normal behavior—everything from how it walks to how it interacts with you. This can serve as a baseline with which to compare suspicious changes.

Visiting Your Service Provider

Barring emergencies, most cats will require a handful of veterinary visits during their first year of life and annual visits thereafter. Listed below is an approximate guideline of when you should expect to have the cat serviced and what you can expect from your veterinarian. Ideally, a kitten's first visit to the clinic should take place before it goes to your home. Follow-up visits should be done as your service provider recommends.

First Visit (8–12 Weeks)

- General physical exam
- Check kitten for parasites (intestinal worms, fleas, ear mites)
- Have kitten dewormed
- Test for feline leukemia and feline AIDS
- If seasonally appropriate, begin heartworm preventative
- Discuss which vaccines to administer and when to give them
- If seasonally and environmentally appropriate, begin flea and tick medications
- Discuss any issues of feline maintenance you may have questions about, including grooming, feeding, litter box protocols, etc.

Second Visit (11–15 Weeks)

- General physical exam
- Have kitten dewormed
- Check kitten for parasites
- Administer veterinarian-recommended vaccinations
- Discuss behavioral problems, if any

Third Visit (14–17 Weeks)

■ General physical exam

■ Have kitten dewormed

■ Check kitten for parasites

■ Discuss appropriate time for spaying/neutering; schedule procedure

■ Administer veterinarian-recommended vaccinations

■ Discuss behavioral problems, if any

■ Discuss transition to adult-formula cat food

■ Change heartworm preventative dosage to reflect kitten's growth

Annually

■ General physical exam

■ Appropriate immunization boosters

■ Deworming (if necessary)

■ Heartworm blood test

■ Wellness testing for mature cats (initiated at 6 or 7 years of age to evaluate kidneys, liver, blood sugar, and other organ functions)

■ Feline leukemia and feline AIDS tests (if the cat accesses the outdoors).

Hardware Glitches

Throughout its life, the average cat will display numerous mechanical "hiccups," most of which it will quickly resolve on its own. If the symptoms persist or worsen over a 24-hour period, however, you should consider seeking professional assistance. Familiarize yourself (and, if appropriate, other members of your family) with the following common malfunctions. Do this in advance, because during a real emergency there will likely be no time to locate and consult reference materials.

Bleeding: Superficial cuts or scrapes can be treated at home. Deeper injuries or puncture wounds (especially if inflicted by another cat) require immediate veterinary attention, as does persistent, uncontrolled bleeding from a wound or orifice. Occasional, very slight bleeding during bowel movements is usually not a serious problem. However, bloody urine or persistent blood in the stool should be investigated immediately.

Breathing Difficulty: Prolonged respiratory distress (coughing, sneezing, labored breathing, etc.) may signal anything from pneumonia to a severe allergic reaction. Consult your veterinarian immediately.

Collapse: If your cat falls and cannot stand up, contact your veterinarian and prepare to take the feline to the clinic immediately. Try to remember what transpired in the moments before the incident; knowledge of these events may be helpful in determining a cause.

Constipation: If your cat is obviously straining to defecate but accomplishing nothing, contact your veterinarian immediately. This could indicate such life-threatening disorders as intestinal blockage. Observe carefully, because the inability to urinate is often confused with constipation.

Diarrhea: A brief bout can be brought on by something as minor as a dietary change. If the problem persists for 24 hours, contact your veterinarian. Prolonged bouts can lead to dehydration.

Ear Discharge: Healthy felines generate a small amount of waxy discharge. If this output becomes excessive, takes on a new color, or develops a bad odor, consult your veterinarian. The same advice applies if the feline periodically shakes its head or continually scratches its ears.

Excessive Water Consumption: This can be an indicator of diabetes (common in overweight cats) or kidney malfunction.

Eye Discharge: A certain amount of discharge from the eyes (particularly in longhaired models) is normal. Excessive and/or discolored discharge should be reported to your veterinarian. Virtually any eye difficulty (redness, swelling, irritation, etc.) should be reported, and all eye injuries (foreign objects, scratches) require immediate professional attention.

Fever: The temperature range of a normal cat is 100°F to 102.5°F (37.7–39°C). This can go slightly higher on very hot days. Contact your veterinarian if your feline's temperature is below 99°F (37°C) or above 103°F (39.5°C). (See "Measuring the Cat's Core Temperature," page 169.)

Grooming (Neglect of): Cats are hardwired to groom themselves. A feline that suspends this behavior is almost always in distress. If your feline stops grooming for any noticeable length of time, seek professional advice.

Gum Discoloration: Pink gums indicate normal oxygenation of the gum tissue. Pale, white, blue, or yellow gums require veterinary attention. To make a crude assessment of your feline's circulation, press on the gums and release. Ideally, the pink coloration should return within 1 or 2 seconds. If it takes less than 1 second—or more than 3 seconds—for the area to return to its normal pink color, some sort of vascular disorder may be responsible.

Limping (Persistent): If the problem persists for more than an hour or two, consult a veterinarian. Any change in a cat's normal movements (slowing down, sudden refusal to jump, change of gait, and so on) should be monitored and, if it persists, brought to the attention of your veterinarian.

Loss of Appetite: Can denote anything from dissatisfaction with a particular food to infectious disease or severe pain. The first step is to see if something about the feline's feeding ritual (the food, its bowls, the place where the meal is offered) has changed. However, if the behavior continues for 24 hours, seek professional help.

Pain: If your cat is in obvious pain, seek medical help immediately. Cats are extremely skilled at hiding their discomfort. If a feline can no longer accomplish this, it is probably experiencing severe malfunction.

Seizures: Could signal any number of malfunctions, from poisoning to a severe head injury. Remain with the cat during the episode and, if possible, time how long it lasts. Once it passes, consult your veterinarian. If the seizure continues for longer than 5 minutes, transport the cat (if necessary, while still seizing) to the veterinary office. To avoid injury, wear protective clothing (long sleeves, gloves) while handling the feline. Also, try to remember what transpired just before the attack; knowledge of these events may be helpful in determining a cause.

Skin Irritation: Any development of scabs, redness, excessive itching, or localized hair loss should be professionally assessed.

Tremors: Can indicate anything from neurological disease to fever. Consult your veterinarian immediately.

Urination (Inability to): Contact your veterinarian immediately. This can indicate an acute, dangerous malfunction, such as blockage of the urinary tract or renal failure.

Urination (Inappropriate): Stress can cause cats to "miss" the litter box. However, it can also be a sign of serious illness—especially if the problem involves more than one or two isolated incidents. In a non-neutered male, urinating outside the litter box may constitute a territorial marking behavior.

Urination (Painful): Trouble with liquid expulsion is one of the key signs of urinary tract infection and/or obstruction. Consult your veterinarian immediately.

Vomiting: All cats occasionally vomit. If the vomiting becomes regular, does not take place shortly after meals, or is not obviously associated with fur-ball expulsion, consult your veterinarian. Get help immediately if the cat seems to be in pain, attempts to vomit but produces nothing, has blood in its vomit, and/or vomits repeatedly.

Weight Loss: It is a good idea to weigh your cat each week, so sudden weight changes do not go unnoticed. A feline who experiences precipitous weight loss for any reason (a half pound [225 g] in a week) needs immediate veterinary care. Rapid loss of mass, often a symptom of another malfunction, can also be a problem in and of itself; it can cause internal damage in felines. (See "Weighing a Cat," page 120.)

Creating a Home Repair Kit

Most feline-related medical issues should be handled by a veterinarian. However, minor problems can be dealt with at home—and some major problems can be stabilized before transport to a veterinarian's office—using the following equipment. Place all of these items in one container (a small, plastic toolbox is ideal) and position it someplace easily

accessible. Include the name and phone number of your veterinarian, along with the phone number of the nearest animal emergency clinic.

- Roll cotton and cotton balls
- Gauze pads and gauze tape
- Heavy gloves
- Scissors
- Eyewash
- Oral syringes
- Large towel
- Exam gloves
- Surgical tape
- Ice pack
- 3-percent hydrogen peroxide
- Thermometer (preferably digital)
- Pill gun (see page 166)

You may also wish to keep a feline medical file near your home repair kit. This folder should contain all relevant information regarding your cat's medical history, including:

- Information on all immunizations the cat has received (with dates)
- A list of previously taken medications
- Current medications, including heartworm and flea preventatives
- Blood test dates and results
- Owner copies of veterinary office invoices and examination sheets, if possible (these provide a useful "paper trail" of past conditions and treatments)

⚠ *CAUTION: Never give cats medicines designed for humans, except under veterinary supervision. Even mild doses of common, over-the-counter compounds can cause severe malfunctions and/or full system shutdown. (See "Poisons," page 179.)*

Administering Ear Medication

Cats' ears are particularly sensitive—even more so if they are suffering from a painful infection that requires medication. Follow these steps when introducing compounds into the auditory canals, and be prepared for a struggle.

[1] Make sure the medication is close at hand. If your cat is likely to resist violently, wrap it in a towel and, perhaps, employ an assistant.

[2] Place the cat on your lap. Hold it firmly.

[3] Use your dominant hand to drop the required amount of medication into the first ear. Try to drop it straight in (Fig. A).

[4] Immediately fold over the cat's ear with your dominant hand to keep the medication inside (Fig. B). Massage the lower ear with your other hand to help disperse the drug.

[5] Repeat procedure on the other ear.

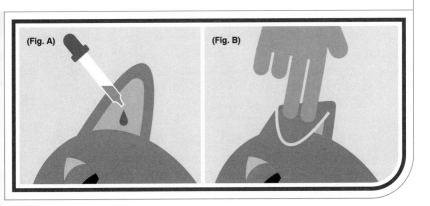

(Fig. A)

(Fig. B)

Administering Pills

If you will be administering pills on a regular basis, you may wish to invest in a pill gun. This device consists of a long plastic tube with a plunger at one end. It is designed to "shoot" a pill directly into the cat's mouth. If you do not have a pill gun, employ the following technique instead. However, be advised that some felines object strenuously to this procedure. To prevent injury, wrap the feline in a towel and hold it firmly.

[**1**] Place the pill within easy reach.

[**2**] Kneel with the cat between your legs, facing out (Fig. A).

[**3**] Using your nondominant hand, grip the top of the cat's head and point its nose at the ceiling (Fig. B). Its mouth should open naturally.

[**4**] Using your nondominant hand, gently open the mouth with pressure from the thumb and middle finger.

[**5**] Use your dominant hand to drop the pill down the cat's throat (Fig. C). Try to get it past the tongue.

[**6**] Gently but firmly close the cat's mouth using your nondominant hand.

[**7**] Immediately massage the throat and underside of the lower jaw to make sure the feline swallows. Blowing on the cat's nose (Fig. D) will also cause it to spontaneously swallow.

[**8**] Release the cat and offer praise and, perhaps, a treat. Monitor it for a few moments for signs of immediate regurgitation.

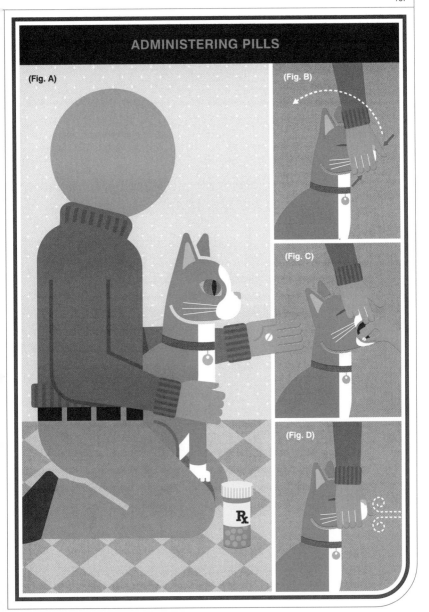

ADMINISTERING PILLS

(Fig. A)

(Fig. B)

(Fig. C)

(Fig. D)

EXPERT TIP: *Make sure the cat's prescription contains several extra pills. A few may be lost during the struggle to get them down the feline's throat. Also, some cats are adept at taking medicines, then spitting them up.*

Injections

Interestingly, many felines object far less strenuously to shots than to pills. Perhaps this is because cats are famously tolerant of pain, yet just as famously intolerant of indignity. In many cases a cat who will spit and struggle against a pill will sit quietly for a subcutaneous (below-the-skin) injection. If your cat is resistant to pills, ask your veterinarian if the necessary medication is available via injection—and if it is safe and appropriate to administer it at home. If it is, your vet can demonstrate the relatively simple injection technique.

Measuring the Cat's Heart Rate

A normal feline's pulse can range from 140 to 220 beats per minute. If it falls outside this range (or if the cat's heartbeat is irregular) contact your veterinarian immediately.

[1] Encourage the cat to lie down on its right side.

[2] Feel for the cat's heartbeat by placing a hand over its left side, beginning behind the front leg. You may also use a stethoscope.

[3] Count the number of beats in 15 seconds.

[4] Multiply the number of beats by four to calculate the beats per minute.

Measuring the Cat's Core Temperature

Use a digital thermometer. Human ear thermometers are incompatible with the structure of the feline auditory canals.

[1] Have an assistant hold the cat firmly (Fig. A). For added protection, wrap the cat in a towel (though, of course, do not cover the waste port).

[2] Lubricate the thermometer with petroleum jelly or some other commercial lubricant (Fig. B).

[3] Raise the cat's tail and insert the thermometer about 1 inch (2.5 cm) into the rectum (Fig. C). Hold it in place until the thermometer beeps.

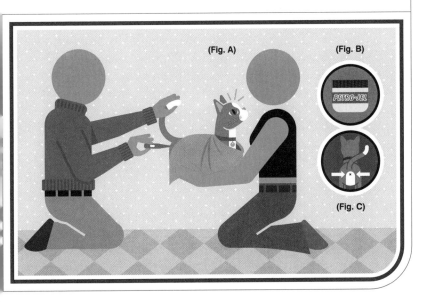

(Fig. A)   (Fig. B)

PETRO-JEL

(Fig. C)

Feline-to-Human Disease Transmission

Though this is not a common problem, a small number of illnesses (called zoonoses) can be transmitted from cats to people, and an even smaller number of human illnesses can be aggravated by felines. This is rarely a concern for healthy adults; however, in some circumstances it can be of special concern to pregnant women, children, and the immunosuppressed.

Allergies: In general, allergic reactions to cats (Fig. A) are more severe than those to dogs. This is because the cat literally coats itself during grooming with *Fel d1*, the enzyme in its saliva that triggers the human allergic response. This substance is spread not by shed hair, but by near-microscopic skin flakes called dander. Cat allergies can be severe, even life-threatening, for people with asthma. Those with mild symptoms may be able to manage the problem with drugs, regular housecleaning, and a rigorous cat grooming program.

Cat Scratch Disease: There has been considerable debate on this subject, but most believe this disease is caused by the *Rochalimaea henselae* bacteria; it is transmitted from cats to humans via bites and scratches. It is also carried by fleas. The disease can cause flu-like symptoms and lymph node lesions. In healthy individuals antibiotics are sufficient to treat it. However, cat scratch disease can play havoc with the immunosuppressed.

Chlamydia: A strain of the same type of bacterium that causes disease in humans, this variety can trigger respiratory infections in cats. If contracted by humans, it can trigger a similar illness that, if left untreated, may develop into pneumonia. However, the danger of cat-to-human transmission is almost nonexistent for anyone but the immunosuppressed.

Pasteurella: An infectious bacterium carried in the mouths of most cats. For this reason, cat bites that break the skin should be cleaned and watched carefully for signs of infection. Pasteurella causes pus formation, swelling, and inflammation. Antibiotics will clear up the problem.

Ringworm: This fungal infection, which causes red, ring-shaped lesions or patches of scales on the skin (Fig. B), is probably the most commonly transmitted cat-to-human illness. A large percentage of felines who contract the disease may become "carriers" who, while displaying no symptoms themselves, can spread ringworm.

Salmonella: The bacteria responsible for this disease can be shed in cat feces (Fig. C), and it is most common in felines that catch wild birds. Routine hand-washing after litter box changes will usually make transmission impossible.

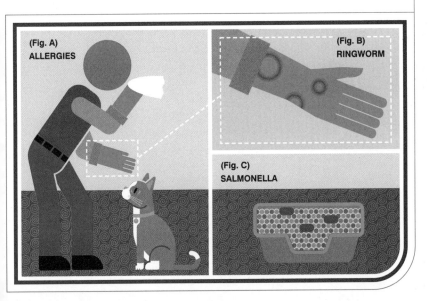

(Fig. A) ALLERGIES

(Fig. B) RINGWORM

(Fig. C) SALMONELLA

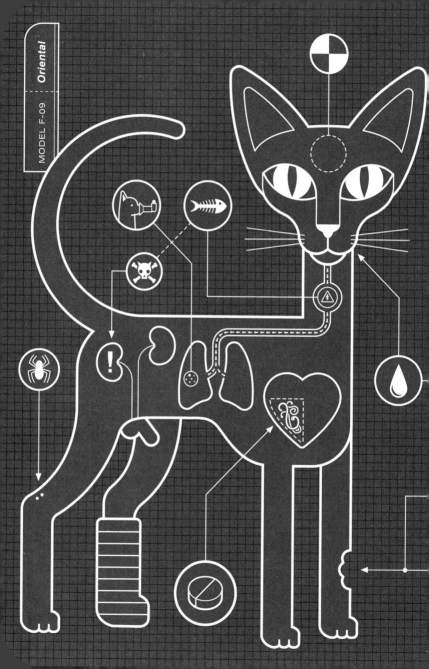

MODEL F-09 **Oriental**

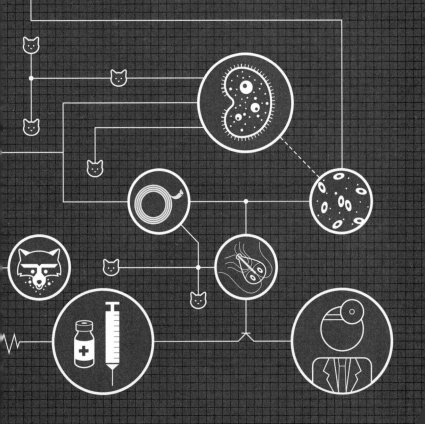

[Chapter 9]

Emergency
Maintenance

Contagious Diseases

Vaccines are available for many of these disorders and should be administered on whatever schedule your veterinarian recommends, based on your cat's potential for exposure. In the case of diseases for which there is no cure, the best approach is to make sure your cat remains indoors, away from potentially infected animals. Be aware that indoor cats are not exempt from vaccinations. Dangerous diseases can be conveyed to them by their owners or during an unauthorized outdoor excursion.

For quick reference, disorders are flagged with a cross (✚) to indicate that immediate veterinary attention is required. A skull (☠) designates potentially lethal disorders.

✚ **Bordetella:** A mild respiratory infection often found in multicat settings such as shelters and boarding kennels (hence its common name, "kennel cough"). A vaccine exists, but is not recommended for cats that do not live in group settings and are not professionally groomed (where they may come in contact with multiple felines). Consult your veterinarian.

✚ **Chlamydia:** This common respiratory disease causes conjunctivitis. A vaccine is available. (See page 170.)

✚ ☠ **Feline AIDS:** Also called feline immunodeficiency virus, it is the cat equivalent of the human disorder AIDS. As in humans, the disease compromises the immune system, leaving the model open to cancer, viral and bacterial infections, and other opportunistic disorders. There is no cure. Infected models may remain healthy for many years, but they should be kept from contact with other felines. Be prepared to aggressively treat any health concerns as soon as they arise. Feline AIDS cannot be transmitted to humans.

✚ ☠ Feline Asthma: Though not a "contagious" disorder, asthma can strike cats suddenly, even catastrophically, at any point in their lives. Common signs include difficulty breathing accompanied by wheezing and coughing. The severity and duration of symptoms vary among individual models. As in humans, the condition can be managed through medication but not cured.

✚ ☠ Feline Calcivirus: A disorder transmitted by feline saliva and respiratory secretions, it produces flu-like symptoms and can occasionally be fatal to kittens. Cats who contract the disease may remain carriers for years. A vaccine is available that may prevent or lessen the severity of the symptoms.

✚ ☠ Feline Distemper: Also called feline panleukopenia, this is an entirely different malady from canine distemper. This very dangerous intestinal virus attacks the intestinal lining and bone marrow, causing symptoms ranging from fever and tremors to diarrhea, dehydration, and the destruction of white blood cells. The disease is often lethal to kittens (of those that contract it, about 75 percent die). A vaccine is available.

✚ ☠ Feline Infectious Peritonitis: This always deadly disorder is of particular concern in multicat settings, because it is transmitted by physical contact with infected cats or with their food bowls or bedding. The ailment is caused by a strain of coronavirus, other types of which are responsible for much milder disorders in kittens. Unfortunately, testing cannot determine if a cat is infected with a mild coronavirus or the deadly form. While many cats exposed to the virus never develop the disease, they may become carriers. The disorder also impersonates other ailments, ranging from cancer to heart disease to brain disease. Vaccines exist, but are of questionable value. The most effective approach is to keep one's cat away from unknown multifeline environments. Consult your veterinarian.

✚ ☠ **Feline Leukemia Virus:** A dangerous threat, feline leukemia contributes to the development of cancer while also weakening a cat's immune system. Vaccines exist, but they are not 100 percent reliable. Because it is so dangerous, any cat you consider bringing into your home should be tested for this disease during its pre-acquisition checkout. Remember that it is not transmittable to humans; that cats who contract it can sometimes live for years in comfort; and that in some rare cases felines can actually reject it from their systems. For this reason, regular retesting is important (consult your veterinarian).

✚ ☠ **Feline Viral Rhinotracheitis:** An upper respiratory illness caused by a herpes virus that is transmitted among cats by their saliva. It can occasionally be fatal to kittens. The disease may also linger for years in the systems of adult felines, allowing them to infect others. A vaccine is available, though it doesn't make the cat completely invulnerable. It simply lessens the severity of the disease. This vaccination is often combined with one for feline calcivirus (see page 175).

✚ ☠ **Rabies:** A viral infection usually transmitted by the bite of an infected animal, rabies causes severe, fatal nervous system damage. State laws vary, but in some locales unvaccinated pets who encounter rabid animals are euthanized immediately.

Chronic Diseases

✚ **Arthritis:** Debilitating joint inflammation often seen in older cats. The condition can be aggravated by obesity. Mild pain relievers can alleviate the symptoms. Never give human painkillers or arthritis medications to cats.

✚ ☠ **Bladder Dysfunction:** The feline urinary system is heir to a host of disorders, ranging from bladder irritation to urinary tract obstruction (in which the urethra of male cats is blocked by crystals or mucus). In all cases, bladder dysfunction can be very painful for the affected cat. If your feline seems to have trouble urinating, contact your veterinarian immediately.

✚ ☠ Cancer: Cancer in its various forms (especially malignant tumors) is very common in felines. As with human cases, feline cancer is battled using surgery, drugs, and radiation, among other methods. Success rates depend on the type of cancer, aggressiveness of treatment, and how early the problem is discovered.

✚ ☠ Diabetes: As in humans, this malfunction develops when the unit's pancreas loses the ability to regulate the amount of sugar, via the hormone insulin, in the bloodstream. In one form of the disease, the pancreas doesn't produce enough insulin; in another, the insulin doesn't function properly. Obese cats are particularly susceptible to diabetes, which can be treated with dietary changes and/or medication.

✚ ☠ Heart Disease: This can be either a genetic or an acquired malfunction, although acquired heart disease is much more common in cats. Often caused by damaged or malformed heart valves, it is usually diagnosed when a routine veterinary examination reveals a heart murmur. There is no cure for heart disease, but in many cases it can be managed with medication, lifestyle changes, and careful monitoring.

✚ ☠ Hyperthyroidism: Commonly seen in older cats, it is caused by an overproduction of thyroid hormone. This can trigger an uncontrolled increase in the metabolic rate, causing dramatic weight loss and internal organ damage. The disorder can be treated through medication, surgery, and/or radioactive iodine therapy.

✚ ☠ **Kidney Disease:** Chronic kidney disease may occur as the cat ages. The kidneys become less and less efficient at straining toxins from the blood, causing a slow buildup of poisons in the feline body. Cats suffering from this ailment may drink and urinate far more than normal. Dietary changes and medication can slow the disease, but many cats eventually succumb to kidney failure.

Hereditary Diseases

In some cases, specific purebred cat varieties are prone to genetic maladies. However, this problem is not nearly as pronounced in cats as it is in dogs, which have been intensely selectively bred for thousands of years. The problem exists because pairing cats to highlight desirable traits (say, silky hair or an interesting color scheme) can also accentuate undesirable traits. For example, Himalayans are prone to cataracts; some Persian varieties suffer from polycystic kidney disease; and the Manx can experience severe skeletal deformities.

This doesn't mean you shouldn't acquire a particular model—only that you should be alert to its special needs. Talk to your veterinarian about the strengths and weaknesses of various cat models. Also, remember that in almost all cases, randomly bred felines are completely free of the genetic abnormalities seen in purebreds.

Allergies

Allergies are a malfunction of the feline's immune system that triggers an overresponse to specific environmental factors (called allergens). This disorder is as common among cats as it is among people. While humans often experience respiratory symptoms (runny nose, sneezing), allergic felines can manifest dermatological symptoms (scabs, itching, hair loss, etc.) or gastrointestinal complaints (vomiting and/or diarrhea). Unfortunately, cats can be allergic to a great many things, from foods and fleabites to grass. Individual reactions to allergens can range from mild discomfort to life-threatening emergencies (including allergen-induced swelling and constriction of the airway). Food allergies can trigger vomiting and/or diarrhea; allergic reactions to insect bites can be very serious and may lead to a potentially fatal condition called anaphylactic shock. If you suspect your cat is allergic to something in its environment, consult your veterinarian.

EXPERT TIP: *When attempting to trace the source of a feline allergy, try to determine if anything significant about the cat's environment changed just before the onset of symptoms. Some react quite strongly to such environmental factors as the odor of new carpet, freshly painted walls, even the scent of a new piece of electronic equipment. Also, many cats are allergic to plastic.*

Poisons

Cats, with their propensity for investigating new things, may sometimes consume questionable substances. If you see your cat ingest such an item, immediately (if possible) flush its mouth with water to remove any residue. Do not panic, as this will agitate the cat and, perhaps, cause it to retreat to an inaccessible location. Instead, confine the cat to one room and contact your veterinarian for further instructions. Or call the American Society for the Prevention of Cruelty to Animals (ASPCA) Animal Poison Control Center at (888) 426-4435 (4ANIHELP). If you are instructed to visit a clinic, try to bring the toxin's container with you; this may provide vital information about the substance your cat ingested.

✚ ☠ **Acetaminophen:** Just one 500-mg tablet of this over-the-counter painkiller (the active ingredient in Tylenol) is enough to kill an adult cat. *Symptoms:* Vomiting, drooling, blood in urine, and/or brown or blue mucus membranes. *Treatment:* If consumption of the acetaminophen was very recent, induce vomiting. (See "Inducing Vomiting," page 183.) Seek immediate veterinary attention. Be advised that the prognosis, even if help is sought immediately, is very poor.

✚ ☠ **Antifreeze:** Cats may be attracted to the sweet taste of antifreeze. *Symptoms:* Convulsions, wobbling, vomiting, coma, and death. *Treatment:* If you are absolutely certain the cat has consumed antifreeze, induce vomiting and seek immediate medical attention. Even with prompt medical intervention, antifreeze poisoning is often fatal.

✚ ☠ **Aspirin:** Toxic even in small doses, it causes kidney failure, stomach ulceration, and inflammation of the liver, among other malfunctions. *Symptoms:* Blood-tinged vomit, abdominal pain, weakness, and/or coma. *Treatment:* If consumption of the aspirin was very recent, induce vomiting (page 183). Seek immediate veterinary attention. Prognosis is poor if treatment begins after symptoms appear.

✚ ☠ **Lead:** This toxin is often found in old paint chips. *Symptoms:* Poor appetite, weight loss, vomiting, escalating to convulsions, paralysis, blindness, and/or coma. *Treatment:* Lead-poisoning symptoms build slowly over time. If your cat seems to display them, ask your veterinarian to run a blood or urine test.

✚ ☠ **Vermin Poisons:** Felines can be harmed by ingesting rat poison, or even by ingesting rats or mice that have themselves ingested rat poison.

Symptoms: Convulsions, stiffness, hemorrhage, and/or collapse. A common toxin in these products is warfarin, which disrupts the cat's blood-clotting ability. *Treatment:* The best approach depends on the active ingredient in the poison. Obtain the original packaging if possible and seek immediate veterinary care.

✚ ☠ **Zinc:** Present in everything from pennies to sunblock to shampoos, this metal can cause severe internal damage at the cellular level. *Symptoms:* For minor exposures, vomiting, abdominal pain, and diarrhea; for major doses, severe anemia, weakness, jaundice, bloody urine, and multiple organ failure. *Treatment:* Seek immediate veterinary care. Treatment is usually ineffective in high-dose cases.

Other Unauthorized Ingestions

Most pet owners understand the importance of locking chemicals and poisons away from felines. What they may not realize is that many common compounds are also toxic. Below is a partial list of often innocuous items that can cause system failure in cats.

Alcohol: Toxic to cats, even in low doses.

Caffeine: Dangerous to felines. Do not allow cats to access caffeine-laced soft drinks, tea, coffee, or coffee grounds.

Chocolate: The more "pure" the product, the greater its toxicity to felines. For instance, baking chocolate is more dangerous than milk chocolate.

Lilies: All parts of the Easter lily, tiger lily, and daylily, among others, are toxic to cats. Ingestion leads to kidney failure and, if no treatment is forthcoming, death.

 Macadamia Nuts: An unknown toxic agent in this food product can cause tremors, lameness, joint stiffness, and hyperthermia in felines.

 Mothballs: Ingestion can cause life-threatening liver damage, among other problems.

 Pennies: Due to their high concentration of zinc, pennies can be extremely toxic if ingested.

 Pine Oils: This common ingredient in home cleaning products can cause everything from abdominal pain to organ damage.

 Potpourri Oils: If ingested, can cause internal injuries and chemical burns; can irritate skin if applied to the body.

 Tobacco: The nicotine in tobacco attacks the nervous and digestive systems, and it can trigger rapid heartbeat, coma, and even death. Recent studies also assert that cats who inhale secondhand smoke double their chances of developing a form of cancer known as malignant lymphoma.

EXPERT TIP: *The odds of felines ingesting these items may be greater than they appear. Because cats are self-cleaning, they will lick up (and consume) any substance that spills onto, or is rubbed into, their fur or*

paws. For this reason, it is important for you to immediately clean up any foreign substances on your cat's exterior or anything that the feline might walk through. (See "Bathing," page 132.)

Inducing Vomiting

Administer 3-percent hydrogen peroxide, 1 teaspoon per 5 pounds of feline body weight (or 5 ml per 2.25 kg of feline body weight). Repeat every 10 minutes until the cat vomits. Do not repeat more than three times. Never use syrup of ipecac except under a veterinarian's supervision. If mishandled, it can be toxic to cats.

Trauma

Felines, even those that are kept indoors, can incur catastrophic malfunctions triggered by anything from inclement weather to unauthorized, uncontrolled interfaces with canines. In such situations, prompt, decisive action by the owner is the first step toward full recovery.

⚠ *CAUTION: When hurt, a cat's first instinct often is to flee to a safe place—perhaps someplace where it may be inaccessible to you. If possible, secure the cat in a specific location, then speak to it soothingly. Keeping the feline calm and under control is extremely important.*

⚠ *EXPERT TIP: Except in the case of dire emergency or when dealing with an extremely placid, compliant cat, it is often advisable to forgo attempts at first aid and seek professional help as quickly as possible. In many instances, attempting to "help" a struggling, frightened feline will only waste time, aggravate its injuries, and perhaps earn you a few as well.*

✚ ☠ **Blocked Airway:** Airway blockage (choking) can be triggered by traumatic injury, a foreign object in the throat, or a severe allergic reaction. If a choking episode lasts for more than a few minutes, seek veterinary help. (See "The Heimlich Maneuver," page 193.)

✚ ☠ **Broken Bone(s):** Keep the cat calm. Do not apply a splint. If the bone has broken through the skin (a compound fracture), cover the injury with a bandage or clean cloth. If the cat resists, wrap a towel around its entire body to prevent further injury to it or you. Consult a veterinarian immediately.

✚ ☠ **Cat Bite(s):** A cat who is bitten by another cat can face a severe infection and high fever. The bacteria in felines' mouths can cause a runaway infection often manifested as a pus-filled abscess on a bite victim. Fortunately, abscesses are easy to treat with proper cleaning and antibiotics.

⚠ *CAUTION: Humans who sustain cat bites should also seek professional help.*

✚ ☠ **Dog Bite(s):** All dog bites, even if they appear minor, should be investigated by a veterinarian. The crushing force of such a bite can cause severe muscle damage, internal injuries, and infection (usually becoming apparent after 24 hours).

⚠ *CAUTION: All unknown animal bites, regardless of severity, should be investigated immediately by a veterinarian.*

✚ ☠ **Electric Shock:** The feline may exhibit electrical burn marks on its mouth, tongue, and/or feet. Seek medical attention immediately.

✚ **Eye Injury:** Virtually every eye problem, including sudden squinting, copious tearing, and/or keeping an eye shut, merits immediate veterinary assistance. Do not attempt to remove foreign objects (metal, splinters, etc.) on your own.

✚ ☠ **Heatstroke:** Characterized by rapid pulse, panting, incapacitation, and a temperature that can reach 106°F (41°C). Remove the cat from the heat. Place it in a cool (not ice-cold) bath, drench with cool water, or cover with a cool, water-soaked towel. Seek veterinary attention immediately.

✚ ☠ **Severe Laceration with Uncontrolled Bleeding:** Place a clean towel over the wound and then apply direct pressure to lessen flow of blood. Never attempt to apply a tourniquet. Seek veterinary care immediately.

✚ ☠ **Severe Trauma and/or HBC (Hit by Car):** Wrap the cat in a towel to prevent it from lashing out and injuring you. Apply a clean cloth and pressure to any freely bleeding chest wounds. Seek veterinary care immediately.

✚ ☠ **Spider Bite (Poisonous):** Cats, even indoor models, often find themselves in places inhabited by such dangerous arachnids as the black widow and the brown recluse. If you suspect your cat has sustained a poisonous spider bite, seek immediate medical help.

Bugs in the System

A variety of internal and external parasites can invade your cat's systems, compromising performance and causing acute discomfort and, sometimes, full shutdown. Fortunately, most of these difficulties can be ended or avoided entirely through careful maintenance and prompt medical attention.

Internal Parasites

✚ ☠ Coccidia: Single-celled intestinal parasites that, while not usually harmful to adult cats, can cause severe, life-threatening hemorrhagic diarrhea in kittens. Prompt veterinary attention will eliminate the problem.

✚ Giardia: A single-celled protozoan that inhabits the cat's intestine, degrading its ability to absorb nutrients from food. Appropriate, veterinarian-administered medication will eliminate the problem. Humans and canines can also contract giardia, though it is unclear whether it is the same strain.

✚ ☠ Heartworms: These mosquito-borne parasites can grow into foot-long worms that lodge in the heart, causing significant damage to both it and the lungs. Cats aren't as susceptible to heartworms as dogs are, but they can nevertheless contract the disease and die from it. Diagnosis is difficult, and all treatments are extremely dangerous. The best approach is to have your vet furnish a heartworm preventative for your cat.

✚ ☠ Roundworms: These 3- to 5-inch-long parasites lodge in the small intestine, where they steal nutrients from their feline host. It is most common in kittens, who may develop distended stomachs. The worms may be detected in vomit or feces. Left untreated, they can cause great discomfort and, in rare cases, death. Deworming medication eliminates them. This parasite is potentially transmittable to humans.

✚ **Tapeworms:** The eggs of these parasites can be found in fleas, feces, and any "kills" your cat may make while outdoors. Infected felines may seem lethargic, though some betray no symptoms at all. A telltale sign is the rice-shaped tapeworm segments cats occasionally excrete, which may be found in their bedding, their litter box, or on the cats themselves. Deworming medication destroys tapeworms.

External Parasites

✚ **Ear Mites:** These small, spiderlike parasites live deep in felines' ear canals, where they suck lymph from the skin. This is so irritating that an infected cat may scratch its ears raw trying to alleviate the discomfort. Ear mites spread easily among cats. However, the problem can be solved with medicated drops and a regimen of careful ear-washing.

✚ **Fleas:** Though usually only an annoyance to healthy adult cats, fleas can cause life-threatening blood loss in severely infested kittens and already-weakened adult felines. Fleas can cause allergic reactions and even transmit cat scratch disease from felines to humans. Various shampoos, medicines, and topical applications can eliminate small-to-medium infestations. Consult your veterinarian about the proper course of action.

⚠ *CAUTION: Do not use dog-formulated flea products on cats. They can make felines violently ill.*

● **EXTERNAL PARASITES:**

1. **Ear Mites:** Irritate the ear canals
2. **Fleas:** Usually an annoyance, may be fatal to kittens
3. **Ticks:** Can transmit Lyme disease
4. **Treat ear mites with medicated drops**
5. **Use shampoos, medicines, and topical applications for fleas**
6. **Remove ticks with tweezers, then immerse in alcohol**

● **INTERNAL PARASITES:**

7. **Coccidia:** Found in the intestines
8. **Giardia:** Found in the intestines
9. **Tapeworms:** Found in the intestines
10. **Heartworms:** Found in the right ventricle of the heart
11. **Roundworms:** Found in the small intestine
12. **A veterinarian can prescribe medication to prevent or relieve these parasites**

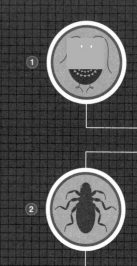

BUGS IN THE SYSTEM: These parasites can invade your feline's system

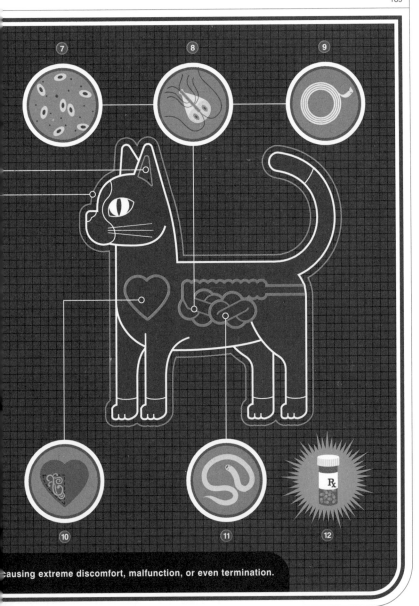

✚ **Ticks:** Because cats are fastidious groomers, they remove many of these bloodsucking parasites themselves. However, ticks may also inhabit such hard-to-reach spots as the top of the head and between the toes. If your cat has access to the outdoors, check the feline regularly for ticks. Remove them with tweezers, then kill them by immersing them in alcohol. Do not handle the ticks, which can transmit such human ailments as Lyme disease.

Behavioral/Psychological Disorders

Not all malfunctions are hardware issues. Some cats may develop software glitches that can be resolved only by specialists. However, disorders so acute that they require professional intervention are quite rare.

Aggression: Problems in this area can include aggression toward the owner, aggression toward other cats, and fear-based aggression. Sometimes this issue manifests itself in the form of too-aggressive play (employing claws and teeth). On some occasions it is driven by an overabundance of prey drive, and it can be stopped or lessened by increased playtime. If the feline's attacks pose a physical danger, however, professional intervention may be necessary.

Depression: The true nature of felines' emotional states can never be known (because they can't tell their owners). However, they can manifest behaviors similar to depression, often in similar situations. For instance, cats who have lost a human or feline companion may go through prolonged mood alterations, sleep excessively, and decrease their food intake. In some extreme cases, cats in "mourning" have been known to injure themselves by refusing, for extended periods, to refuel.

Eating Disorders: Felines who refuse to eat for other than physiological reasons may be depressed or angry. Or they may be extremely finicky—a problem owners can inadvertently initiate by supplying an excessively varied diet. In many cases, the best approach is to stop the problem before it starts by offering a mildly varied but uniform diet. However, if your cat suddenly stops eating or radically changes its food intake, make sure your veterinarian first checks for mechanical malfunction.

Inappropriate Nursing: Kittens taken from their mother before being fully weaned will occasionally try to "suckle" their owners by sucking on skin, clothing, and/or fingers. Very little can be done to rectify this harmless, though somewhat disconcerting, bit of programming.

Obsessive-Compulsive Behaviors: Obsessive behavior in cats often mirrors the same disorder in humans. Affected felines may engage in repetitive actions (excessive grooming, pulling out hair) that seem pointless and even harmful. In some cases, these may be triggered by separation anxiety, boredom, or stress. Treatment by an animal behaviorist may help, as may medication, though often the simplest solution is to pay more attention to the cat. Consult your veterinarian.

Psychosomatic Illness: Evidence suggests that in some cases minor feline physiological complaints (including, but not confined to, stomach upset, bladder inflammation, and persistent vomiting) can be attributed to stress. In such cases (after your veterinarian has ruled out mechanical failure), the best approach is to decrease the feline's stress level.

The Heimlich Maneuver

This technique can assist a choking cat. Be advised, however, that this method can cause serious injury if done improperly, or if executed on a feline with an unobstructed airway. Use it only if you actually witness a cat ingesting (and subsequently choking on) a foreign object.

[**1**] If the cat is wearing a collar, remove it.

[**2**] Open the cat's mouth and look down its throat (Fig. A). If you can see the object causing the obstruction (and if the cat will allow it), remove it (Fig. B). Do not try to remove the object unless you can visually identify it. Cats have small bones at the base of their tongues that may be mistaken for chicken bones.

[**3**] Lift the cat by the hindquarters and suspend it, head down (Fig. C). This is sometimes enough to dislodge the object.

[**4**] As an alternative to step 3, administer a sharp, openhanded blow between the shoulder blades (Fig. D). If neither of these techniques clears the airway, you must perform the Heimlich maneuver (Fig. E).

[**5**] Holding the feline around the waist, press it to your body, as if in a bear hug. Place a fist just below the ribs.

[**6**] Compress the abdomen quickly and firmly with the fist, three to five times.

[**7**] Check the mouth to see if the object has dislodged. If unsuccessful, repeat.

⚠ **EXPERT TIP:** *Even if this technique succeeds, it is still necessary to take the cat to the veterinarian. The Heimlich maneuver itself can cause internal damage.*

Artificial Respiration and CPR

A cat whose respiration and heart has stopped can be assisted with artificial respiration and cardiopulmonary resuscitation (CPR). However, these are last-ditch procedures that should be attempted only if you are absolutely sure the cat has stopped breathing. Place your hand on the left side of the chest to check for a heartbeat (if you find one, the cat is still breathing). Alternatively, hold a mirror in front of the cat's nose and watch for condensation (if you see even the smallest bit, the cat is still breathing). Still another method is to place a cotton ball before the cat's nose and watch for movement in the filaments.

⚠ **EXPERT TIP:** *A cat's pulse cannot be taken at the neck. To monitor the cat's heartbeat, see page 168.*

[**1**] Inspect the airway for obstruction. Check the throat visually, and use the fingers to feel for and remove obstructions. Perform the Heimlich maneuver if necessary (see page 193). Remember that even an unconscious cat may bite on instinct. If clearing the obstruction doesn't reinitiate respiration, proceed to the next step.

[**2**] Pick up the cat. Make sure its neck is straight, but not overextended.

[**3**] Close the cat's mouth, then place your mouth over its mouth and nose.

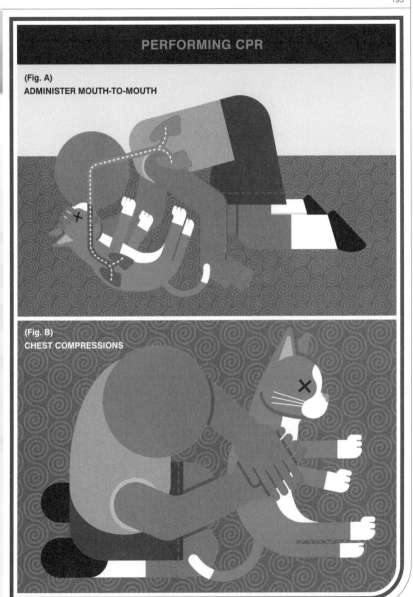

[**4**] Give four or five breaths quickly, exhaling forcefully each time (see Fig. A, previous page).

[**5**] Check to see if breathing has resumed. If not, repeat. Give 20 to 30 breaths per minute.

[**6**] If no heartbeat is detected after 1 minute, continue rescue breathing and initiate CPR.

[**7**] Lay the animal on its side on a firm surface. Chest compressions are less effective on a soft surface such as a bed.

[**8**] Kneel next to the animal. Place palm and fingertips over the ribs at the point where the elbow meets the chest. Compress the chest approximately 1 inch (2.5 cm), twice per second (see Fig. B, previous page). Alternate every five compressions with one breath. After 1 minute, check for heartbeat. If none is found, continue.

EXPERT TIP: *Continue performing CPR until you reach professional help. However, be advised that the chances of reviving an animal with this procedure are minimal. After 20 minutes of CPR, it is extremely unlikely the feline will be revived, even with professional intervention.*

Emergency Transport Techniques

Injured cats should be approached, handled, and transported with extreme caution. A feline in pain may attack those trying to assist it, damaging its intended rescuers and perhaps further damaging itself. The following technique will help safeguard both the cat and its owner.

[1] Assess the scene. For instance, if the injured cat was hit by a car, make sure that the road is clear before attempting to assist the animal.

[2] Approach the injured cat slowly. If it is spitting, growling, baring its teeth, or showing other signs of fear and/or aggression, be very careful. Remember, even a trusted family pet can be dangerous under these circumstances.

[3] Wrap a large towel or blanket around the cat's body. This will permit handling without being scratched.

[4] If the cat is choking or bleeding severely, attend to these problems before or during transport. (See "The Heimlich Maneuver," page 193; and "Trauma," page 183.)

[5] Before transport, if possible, call the veterinary hospital and let the staff know you are on your way. Offer them any essential information you can provide about your feline's condition.

[6] Pick up the cat carefully, trying to keep its body stable. Place inside a pet carrier or cardboard box with lid. Try to keep the feline calm during the trip to the veterinary hospital.

[Chapter 10]

Advanced Functions

FREQUENCY   RECEPTION

Following the information in the previous chapters should give you a healthy, well-behaved, semi-autonomous cat with all the programming necessary for a lifetime of fun and companionship. However, home enthusiasts interested in additional features should consider these options.

Contests

If you would like to test your model against those of other enthusiasts, a cat show is the place to do it. Staged by numerous organizations and ranging from massive national and regional events to small local gatherings, they provide a venue not just for competition but for fellowship and data exchange. The nation's largest such group is the Cat Fanciers' Association (CFA). Each fall it stages the world's largest cat show, hosting more than 1,300 pedigreed cats from around the world. To find out about events near you, visit the CFA show listings at www.cfainc.org.

The cat-show world is very large and complex, so only the briefest overview can be offered here (for more information, contact the Cat Fanciers' Assocation directly). If your cat is a purebred, it must have proper documentation and be a model accepted by the group staging the show. Some associations do not allow declawed cats. Cats are judged on their conformation to a breed "standard" (a sometimes very long list of technical specifications that define, usually in great detail, the model's proper physical characteristics). Pedigreed felines are judged on how well they adhere to their breed standards and little else. Many shows, particularly those sponsored by the CFA, also offer competitions for nonstandard models without papers. These felines are judged on such attributes as beauty, grooming, and personality, rather than adherence to an aesthetic standard.

Shows can be very hectic, intimidating settings for uninitiated felines. For this reason, it is wise to gradually acclimate your cat to such events. A good first step is to attend a show by yourself, to get a feel for the environment. Next, accustom your cat to staying in a "benching cage" (the small metal cages where show cats often spend their downtime) and to being handled by strangers. If your cat does not seem to enjoy or at least tolerate these activities, then discontinue.

EXPERT TIP: *When attending shows, refrain from touching the cats unless their owners give consent. Touching can transmit disease, agitate the feline, or, at the very least, ruffle its carefully maintained coiffure.*

Reproduction

For a number of reasons, chief among them pet overpopulation, the breeding of cats is not recommended by most veterinarians. However, if you own a purebred (some of which are sold on condition that they be bred at least once), here is a brief overview of what to expect during the mating and reproduction process.

Selecting a Mate

Kittens will be strongly influenced by the mental and physical strengths (and shortcomings) of their parents. For this reason, it is important to select a strong breeding partner for your cat. Here are some of the most important factors to consider.

■ Choose a mate from a dependable, experienced breeder. Be prepared to pay a fee for the services of a male cat, or stud.

■ Make sure the mate is Cat Fanciers' Association (CFA)–registered, or registered with another reputable breed organization.

■ Carefully investigate the genetic heritage of the potential mate. Be extremely wary if information about the feline's lineage is not available.

■ Check the potential mate carefully for genetic abnormalities. If there are any questions, a veterinary checkup may be in order.

■ Be wary of any personality foibles, which may be reflected in the kittens. Be particularly wary of potential mates who seem overly fearful or skittish around humans.

■ If your cat is an inexperienced female, pair it with an experienced stud. Likewise, an inexperienced stud is best paired with an experienced female.

Mating

Most female cats go into heat (estrus) three or more times each year. The process seems to be seasonal, with most heats occurring between January and April, and June and September. Cycles are rare between October and December. While each mating cycle lasts approximately 2 weeks, the female is fertile only for 2 to 4 days.

During these key days the female will become receptive to male cats. She will often indicate her readiness by showing excessive affection and by "calling" to potential suitors. When this occurs, the female can be taken to the stud for breeding. The stud should never go to the female, because if placed in a new setting he may waste valuable time exploring his surroundings rather than mating. If the cats appear compatible (the female will make advances to the male, and the male will reciprocate), mating can be allowed to proceed. The stud will quickly mount the female, seize the back of her neck in his jaws, and quickly ejaculate. The head of the feline penis is covered with spines designed to stimulate ovulation; these spines also seem to hurt the female upon withdrawl, so the male will often leap away to prevent being attacked.

Ideally, the stud should be left with the female until she rejects his advances. The pair may mate several times each day.

⚠ *EXPERT TIP: A female can be impregnated by more than one male. In theory, a litter of five kittens could have five different fathers.*

Pregnancy

The gestation period for cats is approximately 9 weeks. The mother's nipples will noticeably redden during her third week of pregnancy. To determine an approximate due date, watch for this phenomenon. The kittens will arrive roughly 6 weeks after it begins. During pregnancy the average female may gain 2 to 4 pounds. Consult your veterinarian about providing prenatal dietary supplements.

Prenatal Monitoring

Your veterinarian can detect a pregnancy via abdominal palpitation at 24 to 28 days and by X-ray at 45 days. A much earlier diagnosis can be made via ultrasound, provided the operator is skilled and knows what to look for. During the early stages of pregnancy some females experience mild stomach upset similar to human morning sickness. This usually passes quickly. Further along in the pregnancy, the female may experience some constipation. Consult your veterinarian if this occurs.

Preparing for Birth

If the pregnant female is not a full-time indoor cat, make it one during the final 2 weeks of the pregnancy. Though in most cases birthing can be accomplished at home, it is wise to discuss the situation with your vet.

Approximately 2 weeks before the birth, provide the mother with a "kittening box." This can be made out of a cardboard box. Make sure it is large enough for the cat and kittens to recline in. Cut an ample opening through which the mother can enter and leave, but make sure it is high enough on the box wall (about 4 inches [10 cm]) so that the kittens cannot escape. Cushion the box with towels, cotton sheets, or newspaper, then place it in a quiet, out-of-the-way location where the female can familiarize herself with it. If she seems to favor some other spot than the one you designate, move the box there. If possible, suspend an infrared heat lamp no less than 3 feet (91 cm) above the box.

Birth

In most cases cats can give birth without human intervention. Labor will begin 6 or more hours before birth, when the female retreats to her kittening box. There she will pant and purr. Then, as labor intensifies, the female will experience powerful contractions every 15 to 30 minutes. Gradually the time between contractions will shrink to as little as 15 seconds. Soon thereafter, the first kitten will emerge, encased in a membrane sac. Once birth is accomplished, the mother will tear open the membrane, chew through the umbilical cord, and vigorously lick the kitten to stimulate respiration. Shortly after the birth of each kitten, its individual placenta will also pass. At the end of birthing, it is important that all kittens suckle. In this first batch of milk, or colostrum, they will receive vital antibodies and nutrients.

⚠ **CAUTION:** *Inexperienced mothers may not chew open the membrane or cut the umbilical cord, so be prepared to offer assistance.*

Feline Transport

When traveling with your cat, use the following handling guidelines to minimize damage and distress to your model. Remember, however, that most felines would prefer to stay home. If this is possible, consider hiring a pet nanny to watch your feline while you travel.

Automobile Travel

When transporting your feline by car, secure it in a purpose-designed pet carrier. Because many cats are extremely averse to automobile transport, it is wise to show them the carrier several hours in advance of a trip, so they can get used to it. Depending on your cat's demeanor, you might also wish to confine it to a specific area before the journey (making sure it has access to water and litter) so that it doesn't attempt to hide.

Line the crate with a familiar blanket and then place the cat inside. This task can either be simple or difficult, depending on how much the cat despises automobiles. Be advised that the cat may vocalize steadily during the entire journey. If you are not sure how your model will react to a long trip, try taking it on several shorter ones. This will give you an idea of its temperament, and, perhaps, will accustom the cat to the novel situation.

If the trip will last more than 1 hour, take along water and a small litter box for the feline to use. At regular intervals, pull the car over, secure all windows, and allow the feline the run of the interior (and use of its litter box). Do not allow the cat to roam the inside of the car, unrestrained, while the vehicle is in motion. This is an invitation to an automobile accident.

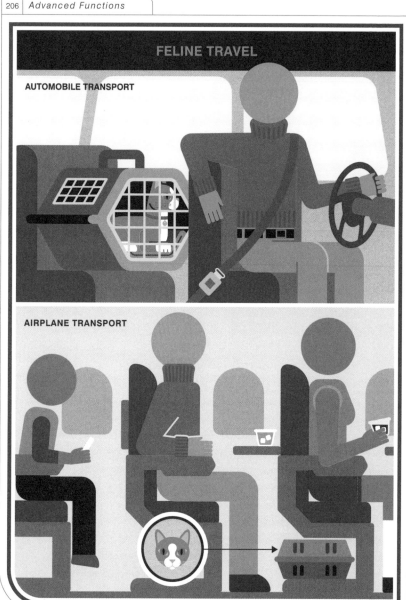

⚠️ *CAUTION: Never, for any reason, leave your cat alone in a car. The interior of a parked vehicle can quickly reach intolerable temperatures, triggering stress, hyperthermia, heat exhaustion, and worse.*

Air Travel

Air travel with a feline is only a good option if the cat is permitted to fly in the cabin, secured inside a travel carrier that fits under your seat (an industrywide airline practice). Unfortunately, new regulations have made this more difficult, with cats often relegated to the aircraft's hold—a rough, frightening, and potentially dangerous place. The environment is extremely uncomfortable, and the cat could die of overheating in the event of a long flight delay. There is also the danger of the carrier being misrouted to the wrong destination.

For this reason, air transport in the hold should be avoided. If you have no choice but to use this system, familiarize yourself with the airline's pet transportation protocols well in advance of the flight. If you don't already own one, procure an airline-approved shipping kennel and make sure all necessary paperwork is completed. Try to select a nonstop flight and, if possible, do not fly during the hottest (or coldest) part of the day. Travel on the same flight as your cat, if possible, and inform at least one flight attendant and the pilot that your feline is in the hold. Provide the cat with a small meal and water approximately 2 hours before placing it in its carrying case. Of course, it should also visit its litter box shortly before boarding.

⚠️ *CAUTION: Veterinarians can prescribe tranquilizers for use during travel, but this will place your cat under the influence of an unfamiliar drug while stowed in the hold, far from help should something go wrong. Discuss the risks and benefits with your veterinarian before proceeding.*

⚠️ **CAUTION:** *Short-muzzled varieties such as Persians should not, under any circumstances, be transported in the hold of an aircraft. Their facial structure compromises their breathing ability under the best of circumstances, so asking them to endure the atmosphere of a cargo hold is out of the question.*

Old Age

Barring catastrophic injury or illness, most feline models age very gracefully. So gracefully, in fact, that the casual observer might not be able to tell the difference between a 15-year-old feline and a 5-year-old model. Nevertheless, genetic and environmental factors make a certain amount of system degradation inevitable.

Felines aged 10 years or older are considered to be "seniors." However, the onset of old age doesn't mean that an endless series of malfunctions is in store. To head off problems, it is important to monitor the feline's appearance and behavior and also to schedule regular maintenance inspections with your veterinarian (some recommend twice-a-year visits for older felines). Older cats exercise less and thus need fewer calories, yet their less-efficient metabolism also requires a higher-quality fuel.

Common Age-Related Malfunctions

■ Gradual decline in auditory sensors

■ Degradation of close-up visual acuity (though distance vision often remains unaffected)

■ Bowel sluggishness and constipation

■ Degradation of liver and kidney function

■ Hair whitening

■ Gradual weight decline and muscle-mass loss

- Propensity for urinary tract disorders
- Increased susceptibility to stress
- Increased sleeping
- Gradual degradation of mobility and motor skills

Obsolescence and Deactivation

Contrary to popular belief, felines do not have "nine lives." However, the service period of individual units can be quite impressive, especially when compared with other consumer items. Properly cared for models will often remain in good order for 15 years or longer. But even though your cat will almost certainly outlast your car, television, and computer, its time with you may still seem startlingly, even heartbreakingly, brief.

This is because while an obsolete car, television, or computer can be discarded and quickly forgotten, a feline cannot. Cats serve more than a utilitarian function; they are also our companions, friends, and family. When the time approaches to part with that friend, owners may feel great trepidation. Yet, this is also the time when they can render their greatest service to a loyal feline companion.

No two situations are alike, but in most cases an elderly feline should be maintained for as long as it remains in relatively good health and free of severe, chronic pain. Fortunately this is often the case almost to the end of the cat's service life. A geriatric cat may not jump as high or play as hard as it once did, but its cognitive and motor skills will remain more than sufficient for semi-autonomous function. Even better, the feline will be perfectly content with its changed circumstances. Nothing in the cat's vast programming base corresponds to the human emotions of regret and painful nostalgia. In other words, an elderly cat does not fret over days gone by and days to come. It lives solely for the here and now.

That fact is very important when considering how to handle a feline's final days. In some cases an elderly cat will deactivate at a time and place of its own choosing. But in situations where declining health incapacitates the cat or causes it to suffer, the owner must act on its behalf. For instance, felines suffering from a terminal illness can in many cases receive "hospice" care, in which the owner takes over (under a veterinarian's supervision) the animal's pain management. There is no attempt to address the underlying (untreatable) cause—only to alleviate discomfort and allow the feline to meet its end in a caring environment, at home.

When the pain and disability in a cat's life seem to outweigh the pleasure, and when there is no reasonable hope of recovery, euthanasia should be considered. This procedure is painless and can be performed at the veterinarian's office or, sometimes, at home. At the appropriate time the cat receives an overdose of anesthetic that causes almost immediate unconsciousness, followed instantly by death.

Coping with the deactivation of a feline companion can be difficult. In some cases, the mourning period may be as long as that for a human. There is nothing unnatural about such feelings. National and local grief counseling groups are available to help bereaved cat owners through this period. Check the Internet or consult your veterinarian for more information.

Rest assured that, given enough time, the pain of loss will pass. It will be replaced by many happy memories, the warranty for which will never expire.

[Appendix]

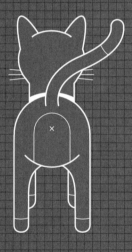

Troubleshooting

For easy access, this section contains answers to frequently asked questions about common feline behavior issues, malfunctions, and quirks. When problems arise with your model, this should be the first place you look.

MALFUNCTION	CAUSE AND SOLUTION
Cat gets stuck in trees.	A trick of physiology makes it very easy for cats to climb trees but difficult for them to climb down. During ascent the feline uses its powerful hindquarters and inward-curving claws to gain altitude. But during descent it must rely on its weaker forelimbs, and its claws point in the wrong direction to be of use. However, it is unnecessary to call the fire department if your feline climbs a tree. Its finely tuned sense of balance will save it from falling. In time it will escape on its own—often by backing down rump first.
Cat kills mice and/or birds, then brings them home to you.	Cats don't recognize pack structures, but they may regard an owner as family. As such, they may choose to honor you by having you share in a kill. The best approach is to not make a scene. Simply dispose of the carcass and then refrain from allowing your cat to roam outdoors unescorted.
Cat seems to make a point of pestering visitors who fear or dislike felines, yet ignores guests who love cats.	People who like cats tend to stare at them. Unfortunately, an unflinching stare is considered an aggressive challenge in the feline world. Thus, cats may shy away from people who pay them too much attention. Conversely, they may gravitate toward those who don't make eye contact—even if they avoid doing so because they cannot stand the sight of cats.

MALFUNCTION	CAUSE AND SOLUTION
Cat seems to loathe your new human love interest.	Having a cat disapprove of your new boyfriend/girlfriend is not uncommon. Neither is having it register its dissatisfaction in very unsubtle ways (snarling, perhaps even urinating on his/her possessions). However, the feline can be won over. Place one of the newcomer's unwashed pieces of clothing near the cat's food bowl, so the feline can familiarize itself with the new scent. Or wear an article of the love interest's clothing while you hold the cat. Have the person in question feed the cat or play with it in a non-threatening way. All of these techniques can create a bond of friendship—or at the very least, tolerance.
Cat climbs drapes.	Try securing the drapes with tension rods, which will fall on the cat if it attempts to climb. Once the cat discovers this, it will in most cases discontinue the behavior.
Cat chews electrical cords.	For obvious reasons, this behavior must be stopped immediately. Coat the cord with a disagreeable substance, such as Tabasco sauce, orange or lemon peel, or Bitter Apple (a commercial animal repellant). If the problem persists, enclose the cord in a heavy casing (available at electronics stores).
Cat hides its food.	When they finish eating, some felines "camouflage" their food bowls by covering them with a piece of cloth, paper, or some other item. This is probably a bit of leftover programming from the cat's wild ancestors, who concealed half-eaten kills so they could return to them later.

MALFUNCTION	CAUSE AND SOLUTION
Cat meows, moans, howls, and makes other sounds constantly, seemingly for no particular reason.	Cats may engage in "hypervocalization" for a number of reasons. Some breeds, such as the Siamese, are hard-wired to make a tremendous racket. In such cases, the phenomenon simply must be accepted. However, formerly quiet cats who suddenly mount sonic assaults on their owners could be suffering from any of a number of software or hardware glitches. An unspayed female will "call" for mates when in season, and an unneutered male may cry out in response. Other causes range from brain tumors to cognitive dysfunction to physical pain. However, in most cases, the cat is probably doing it for attention. Consult your veterinarian if the problem persists.
Cat prefers to drink running rather than standing water and makes a habit of lapping at running or leaking faucets.	Felines may be genetically programmed to prefer running over standing water, which they might perceive as "fresher." For this reason, several retailers now offer running drinking fountains designed especially for felines. Many cats perceive these gurgling fountains as a source of "fresh" water.
Cat chews or sucks on wool and other fabrics.	This curious, relatively common feline behavior may be caused by anything from genetic predisposition (Siamese seem particularly prone to it) to boredom. Felines may be attracted to wool garments because they smell and feel like prey. If the cat ingests pieces of the garment, or if the behavior is disruptive, the best approach is to simply deny the materials to your feline.

MALFUNCTION	CAUSE AND SOLUTION
Cat meows, but no sound comes out.	This phenomenon is called a "silent meow." However, it is silent only to humans. The feline is indeed vocalizing, but at an auditory frequency too high for you to hear.
Cat scoots its hindquarters on the floor.	The cat's anal glands may be full or impacted and may need to be manually emptied. This simple procedure can be performed at your veterinarian's office. If you ignore this behavior, the impacted anal glands can rupture.
Cat seems to hate your taste in music.	While some felines show no interest in music, others may react in strong, negative ways to certain performers and/or genres. For instance, cats who loathe sudden noises tend to dislike rock music. Also, many cats are irritated by high notes, which resemble the distress cries of kittens. If your cat seems to become agitated when you play a favorite CD, turn it off—or at least turn it down.
Cat obsessively bites its nails.	In many cases, this behavior is directly analogous to the human habit of nervous nail-biting. Check for stress factors in the feline's environment and try to lessen or eliminate them. This may solve the problem.
Cat sleeps in an inappropriate spot, such as a bathroom sink, kitchen cabinet, or clothes hamper.	First, make the spot inaccessible or undesirable by securing it in some way. Next, make sure to offer another attractive location for the cat to rest. Position a comfortable bed there and perhaps use treats and/or catnip as an initial enticement.

MALFUNCTION	CAUSE AND SOLUTION
Cat digs up and/or defecates in potted plants.	Try covering the soil surface of the plant pot with aluminum foil, then surround the pot itself with sheets of foil (cats dislike the texture). Never use mothballs (which repel cats) as a deterrent. The active ingredient, naphthalene, is toxic to felines.
Cat actively solicits petting, then hisses, scratches, and/or runs away after only a few seconds of contact.	This behavior is possibly caused by the cat's conflicted views on interfacing with humans. On the one hand, being petted is pleasant. On the other, it is a highly unnatural behavior that the adult cat's programming rebels against. In some felines this quandary manifests itself by first inviting contact, then emphatically rejecting it. The best approach is to pet the cat when it seems amenable, then break off contact at the first sign of a mood change.
Cat eats grass.	The cat may extract nutrients from the greens, or it may eat them to aid digestion. Whatever the reason, moderate grass consumption is natural and not dangerous—with two caveats. Do not allow an indoor cat to chew on houseplants (many are toxic), and do not allow a feline to dine on lawns that were recently chemically treated.
Cat displays complete lack of autonomous function, refuses to clean itself, and displays subpar intelligence.	Consult your veterinarian. You may have accidentally acquired a dog.

Technical Support

The following organizations offer valuable information and/or services to cat owners.

 Animal Poison Control Center (888) 426-4435

Run by the American Society for the Prevention of Cruelty to Animals (ASPCA), the Animal Poison Control Center is staffed 24 hours a day, 7 days a week by veterinarians. They can advise during poison emergencies, provide treatment protocols, and even consult with clients' personal veterinarians. There may be a $45 charge for the service, depending on the circumstances, so have your credit card ready.

American Animal Hospital Association Member Service Center
(800) 883-6301
www.healthypet.com
Can provide information on AAHA-approved veterinary hospitals in your area.

AKC Companion Animal Recovery
(800) 252-7894
E-mail contact: found@akc.org
A 24-hour hotline to which owners of pets with microchip identification can report their lost animals and/or receive information about their whereabouts.

American Society for the Prevention of Cruelty to Animals
(212) 876-7700
www.aspca.org
Founded in 1866, the ASPCA is the oldest humane organization in the Western Hemisphere. Among many other things, it provides humane education, advice on obtaining medical services, and support for animal shelters.

American Veterinary Medical Association
(847) 925-8070
www.avma.org
A not-for-profit association of roughly 70,000 veterinarians that can provide information on AVMA-accredited facilities in your area.

The Cat Fanciers' Association
(732) 528-9797
www.cfainc.org
The world's largest organization for pedigreed cats, the CFA offers data on breeds and primers on feline maintenance. They also sponsor numerous cat shows throughout the year.

Humane Society of the United States
(202) 452-1100
www.hsus.org
Animal advocacy and information clearinghouse covering such topics as pet adoption, care, and rights.

National Pesticide Information Center
(800) 858-7378
www.npic.orst.edu
Offers free information about the toxicity of common compounds such as lawn-care and gardening products.

Petswelcome.com
Extensive Internet site offering comprehensive information on traveling with pets, including listings of hotels that allow them; kennels; amusement park pet facilities; and how to cope with emergencies on the road.

Glossary of Terms

- **Allergen:** A substance that can induce an allergic reaction.

- **Allergy:** A hypersensitivity in the immune system. Symptoms may vary from minor skin irritation and gastrointestinal disturbances to a violent, sometimes life-threatening reaction called anaphylactic shock.

- **Awn hair:** Short, bristly undercoat hair.

- **Breed standard:** The ideal technical specifications for a particular breed, by which all members of that breed are judged.

- **Cobby:** A stocky, solidly built feline body, of the type seen in Persians.

- **Dander:** Minute particles of sloughed feline skin tissue. A protein found in dander and in cat saliva can cause allergic reactions in humans.

- **Down hair:** Soft hair located close to the skin for warmth.

- **Estrus:** Period when the female cat is in heat.

- **Feral:** A cat of domestic origin that has been born and raised in the wild and has never known human contact.

- **Guard hair:** Long, coarse hair that comprises most cats' outer coat.

- **Jacobson's organ:** A sensory organ located in the roof of a feline's mouth that can detect the sexual states of other cats.

- **Mechanoreceptor:** A specialized sensory organ, located at the base of individual feline coat hairs, that can register such things as physical contact and wind direction.

- **Neuter:** To sterilize a male cat via removal of the testicles.

- **Odd-eyed:** Having eyes of two different colors.

- **Onychectomy:** The removal of the claws on the feline forepaws using a technique comparable to the amputation of human fingertips at the top knuckle. Also called declawing.

- **Parasite:** Internal or external life form that uses other animals (in this case, cats) as hosts. Includes, but is not confined to, heartworms, fleas, and ear mites.

- **Pedigree:** A multigenerational record of a specific cat's genetic ancestry.

- **Points:** The cat's feet, tail, and head. Any cat with a Siamese-like coat, in which the body is a pale color while the points are a darker shade, is said to be "pointed."

- **Queen:** An unsterilized female cat.

- **Spay:** To sterilize a female cat via ovariohysterectomy.

- **Tom:** A male cat, especially a non-neutered male cat.

- **Vestibular apparatus:** An inner-ear organ that gives cats their sense of balance. It allows them to right themselves while falling so that they can usually land on their feet.

- **Vibrissae:** The stiff hairs located on a cat's face—12 on each side of the muzzle—that serve as tactile sensors. Also called "whiskers."

- **Zoonosis:** A disease that can be passed from animals (in this case, cats) to humans.

Index

OWNER'S CERTIFICATE

Congratulations! Now that you've studied all the instructions in this manual, you are fully prepared to maintain your new cat. With the proper care and attention, your model will provide you with many years of fun and happiness. Enjoy!

Owner's name _____

Model's name _____

Model's date of acquisition _____   Model's breed, if any _____

Model's gender _____

Model's coat color _____

About the Authors:

A veterinarian for 25 years and operator of Indianapolis's Broad Ripple Animal Clinic for 22 years, **DR. DAVID BRUNNER** specializes in treating small animals—cats and dogs. His first book was *The Dog Owner's Manual*. He has two daughters, Molly and Kendell, two black Labrador retrievers, Lucy and Noel, and a wonderful cat named Mouse.

SAM STALL is the coauthor of *The Dog Owner's Manual* and *The Encyclopedia of Guilty Pleasures*. He resides in Indianapolis with his cat (and former animal-shelter inmate), Ted, plus three terrier mixed-breed dogs and his wife, Jami.

About the Illustrators:

PAUL KEPPLE and **JUDE BUFFUM** are better known as the Philadelphia-based studio **HEADCASE DESIGN**. Their work has been featured in many design and illustration publications, such as *American Illustration, Communication Arts*, and *Print*. Paul worked at Running Press Book Publishers for several years before opening Headcase in 1998. Both graduated from the Tyler School of Art, where they now teach. Paul was raised by a pair of tough-loving Maine Coons named Sandy and Amesley. They adopted him from the pound at an early age and tolerated his presence in their home. Jude has attempted several times to acquire a feline companion, but Huxley—his Boston terrier—expressly forbids it.